Your Expert Guide
to common problems & how to fix them

Triumph TR2, TR3, TR3A & TR3B
(1953-62)

Your marque expert
Paul Hogan

Triumph
TR2, TR3, TR3A & TR3B
(1953-62)

www.veloce.co.uk

See our other imprints for a great selection of special interest, animal care and children's books

EARTHWORLD
EXPANDING HORIZONS

First published in December 2021 by Veloce Publishing Limited, Veloce House, Parkway Farm Business Park, Middle Farm Way, Poundbury, Dorchester DT1 3AR, England. Tel +44 (0)1305 260068 / Fax 01305 250479 / e-mail info@veloce.co.uk / web www.veloce.co.uk.
ISBN: 978-1-787117-25-9; UPC: 6-36847-01725-5.

Introduction

The launch of the Triumph TR2 in July 1953 marked a distinct departure from the prewar ideas of what a sports car should look like. Gone were the cycle-type wings and running boards typical of MGs, Singers and Rileys, to be replaced with stylish all new enveloping bodywork. With a pre-tax purchase price of only £555 the TR2 set new standards in terms of comfort and competition, and it soon became the car to enter in all sorts of competitive trials, races and rallies.

The story of the TR2 has been told many times, but it's worth recounting that this small sports car improved the fortunes not only of Standard Triumph, but also for many of the people who lived and worked in Coventry at the time.

Less than a year after its introduction, one of these new

Triumphs (OKV 777) finished in 15th place at the prestigious 24-hour Le Mans race, and others competed in the equally famous Mille Miglia (OVC 276) and Alpine Rally (PDU 20). However, it was MVC 575 that really lit the torch for Triumph by setting a new speed record of 124mph for 2-litre sports cars.

With the publicity gained from such international success, demand for the new sports car soared, and nowhere more so

0.1: MVC 575, the Jabbeke speed record car that helped start the TR story. It's now on display at the BMM, Gaydon.

0.2: The success of the new Triumph was jumped upon by suppliers keen to add their name to it. This particular advert was issued by Coventry Radiators.

than in the USA, which was to become the key market for the Triumph TR2 and all of the subsequent TR models.

So what was so special about this little sports car from a company that wasn't exactly known for such products?

Sir John Black, the mercurial boss of Standard Triumph, had seen what MG had achieved at Abingdon and wanted to do better. Sir John had tried to buy Morgan, but just as with the later Ford vs Ferrari takeover, he was rebuffed.

Determined to have a sports car of his own, Black instructed his staff to come up with a design that could be manufactured at minimal cost. A styling exercise by Walter Belgrove produced the prototype 20TS sports car. This featured a bobtail with an exposed spare wheel, but from the B-post forward it looked very much like what would become the TR2. It was said to be an unmitigated disaster from a handling point of view, however, and Ken Richardson was brought in to help redesign it into the TR2 we know today.

It's fair to say that the TR2 was an immediate hit with the public, and demand far outstripped supply. Within two years the car would undergo a series of upgrades to become the TR3, easily identified by its 'egg box' grille. The TR3 was later fitted with disc brakes, a first on a British mass production sports car. Another styling revision came in 1957 with the introduction of a full-width 'dollar grin' grille and revised front apron.

Although it was never officially referred to as the TR3A by the factory, the 3A became the biggest seller of the range, with over 58,000 sold.

The last of the line was the TR3B, of which very few were made, and were for export markets only. Finally, it's worth pointing out that the comments contained in this book apply not only to the TR2 but to the subsequent models up to, and including, the TR3B.

0.3: Not quite the last of the line, but the TR3A was the bestselling sidescreen model.

Thanks

As with my other books in this series I am greatly indebted to everyone who allowed me to use their pictures and/or to photograph cars undergoing work or restoration in their workshops. My thanks, therefore, go to Neil Revington of Revington TR, Simon Watson and Tom Boyd of TR Enterprises, and John Sykes and Craig Mallinson of TR Bitz. My thanks must also go to the late Graham Robson, the president of the TR Register and author of many books on Standard Triumph, and also to Tim Hunt for many hours of proof reading the final text.

Contents

1 The engine

1.1: The TR2's four-cylinder wet-liner engine. This is MVC 575, one of the very first TR2s, fitted with twin internal bonnet locks and the correct rocker cover. The bright blue engine bay is also thought to be original and unique to this car.

The four-cylinder wet-liner engine can trace its ancestry back to the Standard Triumph 2000 roadster and the Standard Vanguard saloon of 1947. There were a number of different versions of the engine, and these found their way into a variety of applications. One version was used in the little grey Ferguson TE20 tractor – which could be had as a petrol-, TVO- or diesel-fuelled unit –

while another was used as a stationary engine to power sawmills or generators and suchlike (the author knows of at least one TR2 fitted with such a unit). The Mk1 Standard Vanguard saloon was also available with a diesel engine variant, and thus became Britain's first diesel-powered car.

1.2: The author's Standard Vanguard commercial converted to transporter guise.

The 1991cc engines fitted to TR2s and TR3s are robust but basic units, and most maintenance and repair jobs are well within the capabilities of a competent home mechanic. All TR2s were fitted with what is now known as the 'low-port' cylinder head. However, racing at Le Mans had shown that significant improvements in head design could be made, so when the TR3 was introduced it was fitted with the new 'high-port' head (see Fig 1.4). Cars fitted with low-port heads are now quite rare, as

1.3: A low-port cylinder head. The rocker cover should be painted black, not chrome.

1.4: The high-port head. The alloy rocker cover is an aftermarket fitment.

many owners of early cars ditched them in favour of the more powerful high-port variety.

The cast iron block has three main bearings, and a duplex timing chain drives the camshaft, which, in turn, drives the distributor and both the oil and fuel pumps via a skew gear. The engine block is topped off with a cast iron cylinder head with two valves per cylinder. On TR2s the valve gear was encased within a black-painted pressed steel rocker cover, but when the TR3 was introduced this became a shiny chrome item. The 'push-on' oil filler cap has a wire mesh insert for breathing, and should be at the front of the engine. If it's at the rear, this indicates that the engine may have come out of a TR4. The flat-bottomed sump is a rather basic pressed steel affair, and houses the oil pick up and pump.

The TR3 used the larger 2138cc engine, but it was still possible to order cars with the smaller 1991cc unit right up until the arrival of the TR4, thus allowing for competition in the under 2-litre classes.

Overall, the engine is a reliable and rugged unit that gives few problems in day-to-day driving. It will seem rather harsh and coarse by today's standards, but that's only to be expected.

Problems with the engine
1 Starting
As long as there's fuel in the carburettors and a spark at the plugs a TR engine will undoubtedly rumble into life. And rumble is the right word as the starter motor appears to make hard work of turning over the engine! This, though, is a misapprehension, for the large starter motor is quite up to the job; it just seems to

1.5: The nearside of the engine. It is advisable to number the coil and plug leads for ease of re-fitting. Note that this is a LHD model.

take time before anything happens. As long as the motor is kept in good condition and all the connections are sound and well earthed you shouldn't have a problem with the starter motor. Although the Lucas item is a much heavier unit compared to the lightweight starter motors on the market today, it's remarkably easy to rebuild, and for that reason alone it is worth taking it off the car and examining on the work bench before buying a new one. Often, all that's required to get a Lucas starter back in tiptop condition is a good clean of the copper armature and some replacement brushes.

Many people, myself included, have fitted one of the lightweight quick-start motors that can really spin a TR engine!

Other starting problems can usually be attributed to fuel or electrical issues, and these are dealt with in the Troubleshooting Guide at the end of this book.

2 Low compression

Loss of cylinder head compression happens very quickly if the head gasket fails, and is usually accompanied by tell-tale white smoke in the exhaust. It can also happen gradually, though, and you may not notice it until it becomes serious. Worn cylinder bores, pistons and piston rings are also causes of low compression, but they can only really be checked by removing and stripping the engine.

A compression tester gauge (fitted in the sparkplug holes) will indicate whether appropriate remedial action is needed. Disable

1.6: Testing cylinder compression. Note the HT lead is disconnected from the coil.

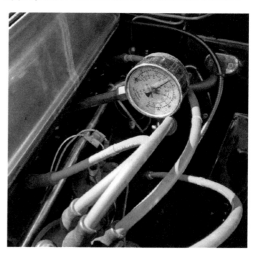

the electrical starting circuit first by removing the HT leads from the coil/distributor – and it's a good idea to put tape on all the HT leads and number them to aid correct plug fitting.

The readings from across all four cylinders should be virtually the same. If one or more cylinders are markedly down on the readings then you may have head gasket, valve seat or valve guide problems.

Low compression can also lead to excessive use of oil, and blue smoke in the exhaust is a good indicator of that. Excess oil getting past the piston rings and into the combustion chambers will mean an engine rebuild is on the cards, and starting will also become more difficult. You can also check the sparkplugs for signs of oil fouling. They should be a uniform grey colour and not black or wet with oil.

3 Cylinder head gasket

A damaged head gasket can be indicated by white smoke (water vapour) in the exhaust. Another tell-tale sign is overheating on the temperature gauge coupled with a loss of coolant. Other indications of head gasket failure are 'mayonnaise' inside the oil filler cap or on the dipstick, a sure sign that water has got into the oilways. However, before doing anything drastic like removing the head, first check that the engine breather pipes are not clogged with dirt as this can affect the running of the engine.

If the head gasket is failing, then you'll need to remove the cylinder head. This is no easy task, though, as you'll need to dismantle both the inlet and exhaust manifolds, and remove the carburettors first. It's a good idea to drain some of the water from the system by removing the radiator filler cap and then using the two drain taps – one at the bottom of the radiator and the other on the side of the engine block just above the starter motor (see Fig 1.7). You can then remove the top and bypass hoses from the thermostat housing and disconnect the pipe from heater valve. Remember to refit the radiator cap to the radiator so as not to lose it!

Once the ancillaries have been cleared away you can then start taking off the rocker cover to expose the large cylinder head nuts inside. It's also a good idea to get number one cylinder to top dead centre as this will make it easier to check the engine

1.7: The drain tap on the block can be hard to reach, and may even be seized. Note the original type starter motor.

timing later on. That can be checked by removing the sparkplugs and by inserting a thin metal probe like a screwdriver into the sparkplug hole. Rotate the engine by hand using the fan until you feel the piston reach the top of its stroke. When that's done you can remove the valve gear, making sure that you keep the pushrods in the correct order. A piece of cardboard with holes punched into it and numbered one to eight will help keep them in the order in which they came out.

When all ten cylinder head nuts have been removed – and sometimes the nut won't come off without the actual stud coming with it – it *should* be a straightforward job to lift the head off the block. Invariably it isn't, of course, as over time the head sticks to the gasket and the gasket to the block. Gently tapping the head with a copper hammer often helps to release the head, but the key word here is gently.

Once the head is safely off you can inspect the tops of the pistons. They should all be consistent in colour. You can expect to see carbon deposits on the pistons, but if water has been seeping into a cylinder then it may look a bit cleaner than the others.

Once removed, inspect the old head gasket for breaks

between the oil and waterways. It's also a good idea to check for cracks in the block and cylinder head that may have led to the gasket failure (see Fig 1.8). Finally, always replace the head gasket with a top quality replacement: it's a false economy to fit a cheap one.

4 Valves and tuning the head

With the cylinder head on the bench you can now inspect the combustion chamber, valves and guides. Valve seats take a lot of hammering, and wear here will be detrimental to the health of the engine. However, if the valves seem okay, then the combustion chambers shouldn't need much more than a de-coke.

If you want to extract more power from the engine then now is the time to do it. Send the head to a REPUTABLE workshop with experience in working such heads. The shape of the engine's combustion chamber can be heavily re-worked to increase power and improve breathing, but do insist that new phosphor bronze valve guides are fitted and then match and gas flow the inlet and exhaust ports to whatever manifolds are to be used. Also, if it hasn't already been done, replace the valve seats with hardened ones in order to work with unleaded fuel. This is another job the engine specialist can carry out for you.

When refitting the cylinder head make sure that the pushrods are properly engaged with the rockers. It is also very important to tighten the head bolts in the correct order. You must start from the centre of the head (see diagram below) and work outward towards each end; gradually repeating the process until all the nuts are torqued to the correct figure of 100-105lbft.

5 Oil, lubrication and cooling

I think it's fair to say that virtually all Triumph engines leak a bit of oil, and the TR2/3's 2.0 lump is no exception. The good news is

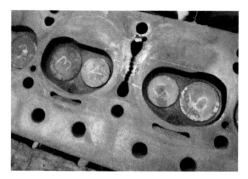

1.8: A severely cracked cylinder head: a common weakness in TR heads. Note the numbered valves.

1.9: Exhaust and inlet valves. Note the different sizes of springs and the bronze valve guides.

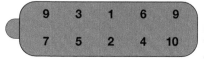

| 9 | 3 | 1 | 6 | 9 |
| 7 | 5 | 2 | 4 | 10 |

1.10: The cylinder head nut tightening sequence, with number 10 at the rear of the head.

that by having a leaky engine you will be topping it up every 800-1000 miles with fresh, clean oil, and what escapes will do a good job of helping to preserve the chassis!

When starting from cold the oil will be thicker, but has to do its lubrication job immediately otherwise the engine could seize. Much has been written about the use of modern versus traditional oil in these types of engines, and the accepted wisdom is that you can't really go wrong with a 20w/50 multigrade oil. However, if you are using your TR 2/3 only during the summer months, then why use winter grade oil at all? Straight SAE 50 will do the job just as well, and should be a bit cheaper.

5.1 The oil pump

The oil pump is driven anti-clockwise by a skew gear on the camshaft. This skew gear also drives the distributor shaft so it's an important component that should not be overlooked for wear. The pump is a fairly simple affair and consists of a pick-up nozzle and an eccentric rotor housed in the pump body. Being immersed in oil they are very reliable units and rarely fail. However, it has been known for the pin that fixes the rotor to its shaft to come loose, with potentially dire consequences. For peace of mind you can fit a rotor and shaft that has been machined from a single billet. For competition work it is also possible to fit an uprated oil pump that produces a greater flow of oil, but on a standard road car this isn't really necessary.

5.2 The oil filter

The standard oil filter is housed in a long canister, which is attached to an alloy take-off housing located just below the

1.11: The oil pump rotor housing and wire mesh pick-up filter.

1.12: The oil pump exposed and in situ.

distributor drive on the nearside of the engine. Care should be taken when removing the canister, so be ready with a container to catch the old oil, which *will* pour out of it!

The filter itself comprises a paper element, a large domed washer, a tensioning spring, and two small washers. It is important to check that these washers do not get thrown away with the old filter. The new filter should come with a larger rubber sealing ring. This sits in the locating groove machined into the alloy housing. Remember to remove the old sealing ring first, which can be done (carefully, so as not to scratch the housing), using a small, flat-bladed screwdriver. Reassemble the canister with the spring, the small washers and the large domed washer

1.13: An original canister type oil filter. This one has been fitted with an oil cooler take-off plate sandwiched between the block and the canister.

in the correct order, and slide the new filter element into the canister. The large domed washer acts as a spring-loaded plate that keeps the oil filter element in the correct position. Failure to replace these parts in the correct order will enable unfiltered oil to pass back into the engine, so do take care in reassembling it. It's a good idea to put some oil into the canister to help prime the system, but don't overfill it. Carefully locate the canister into the alloy housing and bolt it back into position. WARNING: DO NOT over-tighten this bolt, as excessive force can damage the cast alloy housing it screws into.

When all is back in place, top up with fresh clean oil as necessary and check for leaks. If there is a leak from the canister then it's most probably due to the large sealing ring not being seated properly in its groove.

One alternative to the standard filter arrangement is to convert to a 'spin off' canister system. The standard can and separate element are replaced with an alloy adaptor plate and a screw-on filter. It certainly makes an oil change a much less messy affair, and they are readily available from most TR specialist suppliers.

6 Oil pressure relief valve

The pressure relief valve is built into the alloy housing

1.14: A spin-on oil filter also fitted with an adaptor plate for connection to an oil cooler.

that secures the oil filter. It can be adjusted while the engine is running by slackening the locknut and rotating the screw clockwise to increase the oil pressure and counter clockwise to reduce it if the oil pressure is too high. Oil pressure on a good engine should never be less than 40psi when hot at 2000rpm. Anything below that figure and there may be serious problems lurking inside the engine! A figure of 75psi at 2000rpm is much more realistic, but on a newly rebuilt engine you can expect slightly higher figures until it has run in.

The valve itself is a spring-loaded ball, and care should be taken to see that no dirt, grit or other particles contaminate either the housing or the relief valve parts. Low oil pressure will obviously affect the way oil is pumped around the engine, and too little oil being sent to the bearings will rapidly increase engine wear. Conversely, too high an oil pressure can also affect an engine's performance. If it sounds like the engine is knocking or making other rumbling sounds, it could be due to the pressure relief valve having been tampered with in order to get the oil pressure gauge to give a higher reading.

If oil pressure is running low it can be tempting to alter the pressure by adjusting the relief valve but this is likely to prove only a temporary fix as wear will continue inside the engine. Better to trace the fault and replace any parts that need attention instead, but this may require a complete bottom end rebuild.

7 The rear oil seal

The wet-liner engine is fitted with a scroll-type rear oil seal designed to throw any excess oil back down into the sump via the drain hole in the rear main bearing cap. A leak here is not uncommon, but if one is undertaking a bottom end rebuild then a modern two-piece seal can be fitted. There are a number of such conversion kits on the market – Revington TR making a very

1.15: A two-piece oil seal for the rear main crank bearing.

good example – but the crank does have to be reground to accept them. The author has fitted one to his own race car with excellent results, but if you can put up with the small amount of oil that may leak from the standard seal then save yourself some time and money and keep it standard.

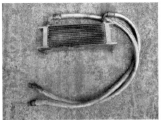

1.16: A 13-row oil cooler fitted with steel braided hoses.

1.17: This oil cooler has been custom fitted behind the front valance. Note the oil feed pipes behind the grille.

Oil coolers

Another topic that is often brought up by owners is whether or not to fit an oil cooler. There are a number of oil cooler kits on the market, and very good they are too. On the TR2/3/3A/3B you can use an adaptor plate that fits between the oil filter canister and its alloy housing, as shown in Fig 1.14. The type of oil cooler used is usually a 13-row type.

Ideally, the oil radiator should be mounted as close to the water radiator as possible, but it'll work just as well bolted to the side of the radiator. However, is an oil cooler actually necessary? If the car gets driven hard or is used in competition then the answer is yes. But on a car that is used only at weekends ... probably not. Research by some oil companies has concluded that oil rarely ever gets up to a temperature whereby it will start to break down. It is, therefore, recommended that if you do fit an oil cooler, then an oil stat should also be plumbed into the pipework, as having over-cooled oil is not a good idea.

Oil change intervals

The driver's handbook recommends oil changes every 6000 miles, but many classic cars today sometimes never cover that many miles in a year. Therefore, If the car is only being used for six months of the year, or during the summer months, then an oil and filter change around March/April time should be sufficient. If the car is to be laid up for a long period of time and in secure storage it's recommended that the sparkplugs be removed and the cylinders sprayed with clean engine oil in order to stop the bores rusting. However, DO NOT attempt to start the car if you have done so before draining off any excess oil, otherwise serious damage to the engine can occur. It is also a good idea to place a note on the dashboard stating 'DO NOT START ENGINE' as a reminder.

Today we are accustomed to driving cars that are quiet and emit very little engine noise. The TR2/3 was designed in another era, however, and engine noise was not only to be expected, but often welcomed as a sign of a powerful car. Rattles, though, are a different matter, and it's fair to say that the early TRs can experience their fair share of them.

1 Valve train noise

Starting at the top of the engine, the valve gear is the biggest source of noise. Rattles here are a sign of incorrectly set valve clearances, a worn rocker shaft, or worn tappets. Valve clearances should be set only when the engine is cold. Cars fitted with higher-lift cams and heavy-duty valve springs can be expected to generate slightly more noise, but it shouldn't be excessive. If it is, then there may be another problem.

2.1: Number the pushrods and valve gear so that everything goes back in the correct place.

2 Timing chain rattle

Timing chain rattle is probably the easiest noise to identify, but not necessarily the easiest to fix. The TR2/3 is fitted with a duplex timing chain for strength, and this enables power to be taken from the crankshaft to drive the camshaft. The chain is tensioned by a flat spring-steel blade, and this is often the cause of noise. If the tensioner is badly worn, the blades of the spring can actually crack and separate at the point where it's located in the timing chest. The blade is held in place by a washer and a circlip, and is an easy part to replace once the timing chest cover has been removed.

Replacing the chain itself is not so easy, as it calls for the removal of the crank pulley. However, with the pulley removed, the timing chest cover can be unbolted quite easily. The locking bolts that secure the timing gears can then be

2.2: The duplex timing chain assembly and tensioner.

undone and the duplex chain removed. Great care must be taken not to disturb the timing of the engine, and it's advisable to use some Tippex/correction fluid to mark the positions of the timing gears and the crank pulley to aid reassembly.

It's also advisable to closely inspect the timing gears for wear, as replacing a worn chain and tensioner won't cure the problem if the timing gear teeth are also badly worn.

2.3: The timing mark has been highlighted on this crank pulley.

3 Crankshaft bearings

The crankshaft and main bearings use white metal steel-backed shells, and these are available in various sizes to allow for regrinding. However, if your TR2/3 is beginning to sound like a diesel engine then you have a problem!

2.4: The three main bearing crank.

It's almost certain that the sound you can hear will be worn big end bearings, either on the conrods or on the three main crankshaft bearings, but probably on both! The noise will be most evident on start-up from cold or when the oil is really hot and thin. The oil pressure gauge will provide you with a visual clue as to the state of the engine, but anything below 20psi is going to be pretty serious.

There are no quick fixes for this: it's an engine-out job and a proper bottom end rebuild. While it is possible to just replace the affected bearing shells it is a false economy to do so. With the engine out of the car and stripped down, that's the perfect time to undertake a proper rebuild in order to make sure the car will be fit for the next 100,000 miles.

With the engine

2.5: With the engine drained of oil and the sump and oil pump removed, the condition of the crank bearings can be assessed.

2.6: Inspecting the bottom end of the engine.

out of the car, drained of oil, shorn of all its ancillaries, and with the cylinder head and timing gear removed, the bottom end of the engine can be accessed. Removal of the sump will expose the oil pump and the three main bearing caps, which, it should be noted, are all numbered, as are the

2.7: Note the F41 number stamped into the block by the main bearing cap.

conrods (see Fig 2.7). The oil pump and the alloy sealing blocks are then removed, and the crank can be unbolted from the main bearings and the conrods. The bearing faces can then be inspected for wear, and, if required, the crank can be sent away for regrinding and Tuftriding or Nitriding.

4 Crank thrust washers

Wear and tear is part and parcel of every engine's life, and the TR2/3 is no different. One of the most common areas of wear is to the crankshaft thrust washer, which shows up as crankshaft end float. Low oil pressure is one of first things you might notice due to worn thrust washers, but you can diagnose this by getting someone to press the clutch pedal while you look at the crank pulley mounted on the front of the engine. If it moves you can bet your life that the thrust washer is worn, and the best way to fix that is to take out the engine.

TR2/3 thrust washers are a two-piece affair which, if worn, can damage the crank face if not replaced. They are available

in various oversized sets, and are fitted to the centre main bearing, being located by a tag on the bearing cap. Make sure that the white metal face of the thrust washer is set against the thrust faces of the crankshaft, and slide the upper thrust washer into position.

As mentioned above, all of the main bearing caps are numbered. It's important that when rebuilding the bottom end that the markings on the caps are placed adjacent to those on the block.

2.8: The centre main thrust washer has a locating tag to stop it rotating and wearing away. It is essential that the white metal side of the thrust washer with grooves, shown on the left, is fitted towards the crankshaft and not against the bearing cap.

5 Pistons and liners

Having gone to the bother of taking the engine out of the car and dismantled the bottom end, it is reasonable to inspect and possibly to change the pistons and liners at this stage, too.

As a 'wet-liner' type of engine, the cylinders can be removed and replaced with larger diameter ones if desired. Original piston and liner sets were graded F, G or H, so it's possible to replace just a single piston as long as it too has a matching F, G or H marking (assuming you can find a single spare piston!). However, historic racing has produced significant improvements in piston technology, so that larger and lighter forged pistons are now used with correspondingly stronger, forged, H-section conrods. With

2.9: A standard piston, conrod and wet-liner. The figure of 8 gasket is available in copper and alloy, and in different thicknesses.

2.10: Compare this standard conrod to the one above it. Catastrophic engine failures like this are rare, but the author knows to his cost how damaging they can be. Standard conrods can be balanced, polished and shot peened to strengthen them.

2.12: A copper head gasket can be easily damaged, so take care to tighten the head studs in the correct order and to the right torque.

such a setup, the 2.2 engine can now safely deliver up to 200bhp, more than twice what Standard Triumph originally quoted.

If you over-rev a standard engine the crankshaft can break in half, and, as Fig 2.10 shows, conrods can be bent and twisted out of shape.

The liners have two 'figure of 8' copper sealing rings (see Fig 2.9) at their base to prevent water ingress from the cooling system, so these must be replaced. The liners also have to stand proud of the block face by 3-5 thou (0.08-0.13mm).

2.11: The wet-liners in position.

While this may seem counter-intuitive, it's important that the correct measurement is obtained, as otherwise the head gasket won't seal correctly.

6 Piston slap

Piston slap can occur when an engine is cold and before it has had a chance to work up to its operating temperature. Often it's a sign of worn pistons, or more likely the piston rings themselves. It can also manifest itself by high oil consumption. If the noise disappears when the engine gets hot it's not something you should worry about, but if it persists and oil consumption is noticeably greater, then an engine rebuild is on the cards.

7 Pinking

This is the sound associated with petrol/gasoline-engined cars with incorrectly set ignition timing. Usually it's because the ignition is too far advanced, and so the fuel has a tendency to 'explode' in the combustion chamber rather than 'burn' as it should. Very high temperatures are generated as a result, and this can lead to valves and pistons burning. Other causes of pinking can be from using fuel with too low an octane rating, a very weak fuel mixture, and an engine that needs a de-coke.

7 Fanbelt screech

If your car screeches like a banshee on start-up, it's a sure sign of a badly slipping/adjusted fanbelt. The original TR2/3 fanbelt was quite a wide item, but many owners have converted the

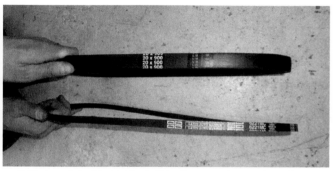

2.13: An original 'wide' fanbelt is shown at the top, but a lot of owners have now converted to the 'thin' belt system below.

pulleys on the crank, water pump and dynamo/alternator to run a thin-belt instead. It's worth checking the alignment of the pulleys and especially that of the dynamo/alternator. They should all be in line with each other. If they are not, and it's usually the dynamo/alternator which is out of alignment, then a few washers on the locating pivot bolt might cure things. Also, when replacing a fanbelt do not be tempted to over-tighten as that can place too much strain on the bearings. A rumbling noise in this area can be from the water pump bearing, announcing that it is about to fail and will need replacing.

8 Chuffing and sputtering

Early TRs are not renowned for spluttering when starting up in the morning from cold, and they quickly settle into tick-over. Once they are warmed up they should perform really well, with the only sound coming from the exhaust. If the engine does cough and splutter then there may be a problem with the head gasket, or more likely from the exhaust gaskets. It's also worth checking the condition of any pipework attached to the inlet manifold for cracks and leaks, as this can also cause spluttering if the fuel air mixture is wrong.

3 The clutch & gearbox

The driveline

1 The gearbox, overdrive and clutch

The TR2 gearbox was originally based on the three-speed 'box found in the Standard Vanguard. Somehow Triumph managed to squeeze a fourth gear into it, but without synchromesh on 1st gear. Gear changing is carried out by a remote selector mechanism mounted on top of the gearbox, and a Laycock de Normanville overdrive operating on top gear only could be chosen as an optional extra. Two years into production the overdrive was made to work on 2nd, 3rd, and 4th gears, and as long as the overdrive is well maintained it offers great economy and effortless cruising. It's believed that about 85% of the cars first sold in the USA were not fitted with overdrive, but if you are considering a TR2/3 from the States then it is a relatively straightforward, albeit expensive, procedure to convert a non-overdrive gearbox into an overdrive one.

Both overdrive and non-overdrive types of gearbox offer four forward gears and one reverse. The ratios are reasonably well placed to provide adequate acceleration through the gears and a decent cruising speed.

Cars that were fitted with an overdrive at the factory

3.1: A four-speed gearbox for a TR2 fitted with an 'A' type overdrive unit. Note the brass oil filler dipstick on the top cover. This handy feature was deleted on later models.

have a letter O stamped on the commission plate, for example, TS6358-O.

During the TR's production run quite a few changes were made to the gearbox, and, to the unwary, one TR gearbox looks very much like another. Some of these changes took place internally and so are impossible to see, for example, plain bearings were changed to needle rollers, but there are some external differences, too. Inspection of the top cover is a good starting point, as early gearboxes have a dipstick oil filler fitted into one of the bosses that was later used for an isolator switch (see Fig 3.1). It should also be noted that gearbox casings from the later TR3B/TR4 are ½in longer than the TR2/3 item due to having a synchromesh 1st gear, but they can be made to fit the earlier models.

Generally, the gearbox in all its guises is a pretty robust unit, but does suffer from synchromesh gear wear, and the main shaft bearings can also wear pretty badly. The top cover holds the selector forks and also the isolator

3.2: This black lump of metal is a vibration damper. Not all gearboxes have these fitted, so don't worry if yours does not.

19

switches for the overdrive. It can also be modified to take a reversing light switch.

2 Removing the gearbox

The gearbox can be extracted from the car at home by anyone competent with a spanner, but it can be a bit of a struggle. Putting the car on a lift or over a pit makes the job so much easier. The gearbox is removed from inside the car, so you'll need to remove the seats, the carpets, and disconnect the electrical connection to the overdrive. The handbrake can stay in situ. With the gearbox cover removed you can now access the bolts that hold the gearbox to the engine and the rear mounting.

Start by disconnecting the speedo cable drive from the gearbox and then undo the four propshaft bolts, noting which way round they are fitted (see Chapter 9, Fig 9.2). The rear gearbox mounting bolts can then be undone and, if fitted, the gearbox exhaust bracket as well. Several of the bolts that hold the bellhousing to the engine can also be undone from inside the car, but others need to be accessed from underneath or from inside the engine bay.

3.3: One method of extracting the gearbox is to bolt some lifting handles to the top cover. However, it's possible to make a lifting crane, as shown here, made by an enterprising Australian TR owner, using a bottle jack and some square section steel.

While underneath the car disconnect the clutch release arm from the clutch slave cylinder, and remove the bracket holding it to the bellhousing. The starter motor also needs to be unbolted and, if possible, removed completely, but doing so can be difficult with the carburettors and steering column in place.

With all the bolts removed from the bellhousing and the engine suitably supported, either from under the sump or with an engine crane, the gearbox can now be extracted from inside the car. Remember, it is VERY HEAVY, and two people may be needed to pull it safely from the car. It's not unknown for the release bearing to fall off its carrier at this point, but by wiring the arm to the bellhousing it is possible to keep it in place.

It's beyond the scope of this book to explain how to dismantle or rebuild the gearbox. My recommendation is to take it to a specialist who can strip it, check it for wear, and, if need be, recondition it

3 The overdrive

Overdrives were common fitments to many cars in the 1950s and '60s, but have been superseded by five-, six- or even eight-speed gearboxes. The Laycock de Normanville overdrive was available as a factory-fitted option on several Standard Triumph models, and the TR2/3/3A series was no exception.

Overdrives allow for easy high-speed cruising at low revs, and also let you trickle along in traffic without revving the engine. They are also prone to malfunction!

The overdrive is operated by a 'push/pull' switch on TR2s, and by a 'teardrop' shaped flick switch on the later cars (see Fig 3.5). These later style switches are quite hard to come by, and although they have been reproduced, at the time of writing they seem to be unavailable again.

The isolator switches on the gear selector cover prevent 1st or

3.4: An 'A' type overdrive unit. Note the lever at the bottom right indicated by the arrow. There is a small hole in the end that should line up with a corresponding hole in the casing. Use a drill bit to check it does.

reverse gear being engaged, while a solenoid on the side of the overdrive itself operates the internal hydraulic pump. With several electrical connections to go wrong the chance of finding a fault increases substantially. It's much easier to check the operation of the solenoid first and see that the control lever moves correctly before taking the gearbox out of the car to fix it.

If all this sounds rather too much to bother with then there is a third solution to the overdrive switch, which was in fact fitted to a number of Belgian-assembled TR2s. An extra lever was mounted down by the handbrake, and this acted directly on the overdrive. All one had to do was to manually push it forward to engage the overdrive. It works in all four gears too! You just had to remember to disengage it and not try it in reverse!

Overdrives require oil to operate properly and a

3.5: The teardrop overdrive switch operates on 2nd, 3rd and 4th gears.

low gearbox oil level will not help things. However, the owner's handbook specifies the use of EP90 gear oil, while the Laycock manual specifically states 'DO NOT use Extreme Pressure oil in an overdrive gearbox.' The author has always followed the Laycock advice and used SAE30 gear oil, with no problems in 40 years of TR ownership.

4 The clutch cover and plate

With the gearbox out of the way, attention can now be turned to the clutch. The TR2/3/3A and 3B all used a Borg and Beck 9in 9A6 dry-plate clutch, bolted to the flywheel and located in position by studs. Removing the clutch cover is simple, but you may need to 'chock' the engine to stop it turning by jamming the starter ring on the flywheel while you undo the bolts. With the cover removed the

3.6 (above right): The six-spring clutch cover as fitted to the TR2/3/3A/3B.

3.7 (right): The clutch release bearing and gearbox oil seal. Note that the bearing has fallen off its forked carrier.

clutch plate can be removed for inspection, but my general advice is to change both the clutch plate and cover for new ones, unless they have only recently been replaced and are showing no signs of wear. The same can be said for the release bearing.

One advantage that this earlier type of clutch has over the later types as fitted to the TR4A is that it can be adjusted through the slave cylinder pushrod. The later TR4A type is supposed to be self-adjusting for wear. That being said, it's quite possible to fit the smaller 8.5in diaphragm clutch to an early car.

5 The clutch release bearing

The release bearing does exactly what its name implies. Pressure on the clutch pedal pushes the bearing forward onto the pressure plate of the clutch cover, thus enabling gear changes. The bearing can rattle, though, and it has even been known to come off its forked carrier due to wear. Check for rattles and replace if required.

3.8: The bearing carrier and locating pin showing where to drill a ¼in hole to aid removal of a broken pin.

3.9: The clutch release bearing carrier. The left arrow denotes the standard locking pin with lock wire in place, and the right-hand arrow shows the position of the additional roll pin. 3.10: The Lockheed combined brake and clutch master cylinder as used on the author's TR2.

The bearing carrier is also a known weak point in the system as the retaining pin can break off leaving you clutchless. The cure for this is to drill a ¼in hole in the carrier so that the remains of the pin can be drifted out (see Fig 3.8). However, a real belt and braces fix is to drill both the forked carrier and the cross shaft and fit a roll pin, sometimes known as a C pin, to it. This was a modification first carried out by Mel Francis on his TR3, and so far it has proved to be a very reliable fix (see Fig 3.9).

Also, while it's exposed, check the seal on the main shaft where it goes into the gearbox. Oil leaks here can contaminate the clutch face and cause slippage.

6 Operating problems

The clutch is hydraulically operated via a slave cylinder mounted on the bellhousing, and this should be the first port of call for investigating clutch problems. Symptoms of clutch failure can be indicated by difficulty in engaging gear or by a noticeably lighter clutch pedal. Both the slave and master cylinders can leak, so it's best to check the fluid levels first. Check for signs of leaking by peeling back the rubber dust covers on each cylinder. Both seals can be easily replaced, but if the bores are worn then the only real fix is to replace the damaged cylinder, but it is preferable to replace both of them at the same time.

The TR2 utilises a different master cylinder to that on the TR3/3A and 3B. The early cars are fitted with a system made by Lockheed, and the reservoir is mounted directly behind the pistons, whereas the later Girling-made TR3/3A and 3B type system uses a separate 'tin can' reservoir mounted to the side of the piston bracket (see Figs 3.10 and 3.12). Both reservoirs

have an internal divider to prevent brake fluid leakage if the clutch cylinder gives up, but, needless to say, the later TR3 Girling setup is a much better system.

7 Clutch judder and slip

A worn or contaminated clutch will sometimes cause juddering as it tries to take up the drive. Worn engine and/or gearbox rubber mountings are also possible causes, and, as these can be easily replaced, it's worth checking their condition first. Replace as necessary.

If clutch slip is experienced when driving, this is usually

3.10: The Lockheed combined brake and clutch master cylinder as used on the author's TR2.

3.11: The bleed nipple in the centre of the photograph is for a concentric release bearing. It replaces the standard setup, and does away with the cross shaft and fork.

3.12: This is the Girling clutch and brake master cylinder setup as used on the TR3s.

attributable to oil or grease getting onto the driven face of the clutch plate. The only sure fire remedy is to replace the clutch plate and investigate the source of the contamination. Oil can gather in the bellhousing from either failure of the crankshaft rear oil seal or the gearbox input shaft seal. Neither is an easy fix, requiring a strip down of one or both components to replace the seals. Incidentally, while petrol/gasoline or paraffin can be used to clean oil from the bellhousing, you should NEVER use it to clean a clutch!

8 The spigot bearing

With the flywheel now exposed it is possible – and advisable – to check the condition of the phosphor bronze spigot bearing in the end of the crankshaft. To do this, undo the bolts holding the flywheel to the crank and remove it. With the end of the crank now exposed you can extract the spigot bush. If it shows signs of wear, a quick fix is to simply turn it around and refit it, but if you can get a new one then so much the better. Spigot bearings should be soaked in oil overnight before fitting.

9 Gear change problems

A badly worn gearbox will make the car difficult to drive. Gears will crunch, jump out, and selection will be difficult. Do not attempt to try to hide this by putting thicker oil in the gearbox, as some unscrupulous owners might do. A gearbox rebuild is the only sensible option. However, one minor irritation may be caused by the gearlever itself rattling, and this can be cured by simply fitting a new anti-rattle spring in the base of the lever.

10 Competition options

One of the easiest mods to carry out is to fit a lightened flywheel, like the one shown here.

It's a bolt-on replacement for the standard flywheel (see Fig 3.13), but if you intend to lighten your flywheel make sure it hasn't already been done, as taking off too much metal will be worse than taking off none at all. A standard cast iron flywheel comes in at around 22lb and can be safely taken down to about 18lb, but you are better off fitting a steel flywheel, which only weighs around 10lb.

For the gearbox itself, apart from upgrading to the Triumph Stag gearbox with its stronger internal parts, anyone contemplating competition could fit close-ratio gear clusters and/or an hydraulic release bearing. The overdrive operating switch can also be fitted to the gearlever if so desired. Revington TR can supply a most ingenious 'logic' switching device that negates

3.13: A lightweight 'spider' flywheel.

3.14: Straight cut gears as used in a dog box are very expensive, and are not recommended for use in a road car.

3.15: This is a close-ratio gearbox as used by the author on his TR3S. Note the lack of an overdrive. It is painted red for ease of identification.

the need to change out of overdrive when changing gears. For out-and-out racing, a dog box can be specified, but they are incredibly noisy, and gear changing can be difficult if you're not used to them.

4 Exhaust & fuel systems

The exhaust system

The standard exhaust system on the TR2 was a straightforward affair that was eventually modified and carried over to the later TR4. It originally consisted of the four-into-one exhaust manifold, a copper/asbestos gasket, a single downpipe, and a short, 18in silencer box placed after the chassis cross frame. Immediately after that was a long tail pipe, which exited under the car's left-hand rear overrider.

Such a setup was apparently rather too loud for the public in 1955, so the silencer was lengthened to 24in, and a smaller, 12in silencer was added into the tail pipe section to further reduce noise. The whole ensemble was finished off with either a chrome or alloy tail pipe finisher.

This twin box setup remained in place for the rest of the sidescreen TRs production run.

The original pipework is made of mild steel, which, of course, rusts. A lot of cars have now had this mild steel system replaced with a stainless steel version made to the original pattern, or with modified silencer boxes. A tubular steel exhaust manifold can also be fitted to replace the original cast iron one.

Starting at the engine end, the cast iron manifolds have been known to crack, which can cause the engine to run rough. Two separate gaskets for the inlet and exhaust ports are used to seal the manifolds to the block. The manifolds themselves are held in place by brass nuts and locating lugs.

The manifold nuts and studs can be difficult to remove, and have a tendency to shear off. If that happens then it's best to remove the manifold itself in order to get at the offending stud. Of course, in order to do that the inlet manifold and its associated fittings also have to be removed.

The middle pipe on both the TR2 and TR3/3A/3B passes through the sturdy box section chassis. Since the rear silencer box is so close to the road it often

4.1: The exhaust pipe runs through the chassis crossmember. Note the way the exhaust pipe clamp has been positioned to avoid the threads being damaged.

4.2: This cast iron exhaust manifold from a TR2 shows the three-stud fixing for the downpipe, and the two studs that support the inlet manifold.

4.3: The cast iron manifold in position. New gaskets would be required, even if just replacing the carburettors.

Wrapping the new manifold in heat insulating fabric is one method, a ceramic coating like Zircotec being a more expensive option. If money is no object then a cast iron manifold can be vitreous enamelled in the same way as those on Mk2 Jaguars. Although you won't be able to see much of it, due to the inlet manifold obscuring it, the black enamel does look good, though it will crack over time. Just don't try using stove enamelling or powder coating as these won't last five minutes.

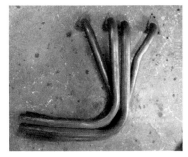

4.4: A tubular steel exhaust manifold. The four separate pipes merge into a single one.

gets hit by speed bumps and the like, so check for dents and scouring on its underside and front edges. The rear mounting bracket can also come adrift from the chassis due to rust or from a perished fabric strap. Replace exhaust brackets as necessary, but, if possible, fit Mikalor exhaust pipe clamps rather than U-bolt clamps, and, when putting the pipes together, wrap the male ends of the exhaust pipes with PTFE tape to aid fitting, gas sealing, and later removal.

If an original cast iron exhaust manifold is replaced with a stainless steel tubular one (see Fig 4.4), it's advisable to fit some form of heat shield between it and the inlet manifold, as the extra heat generated can cause fuel vaporisation and rough running.

The TR2/3/3A/3B fuel system

The TR2/3/3A and 3B use a relatively simple fuel system, which, by and large, doesn't give too many problems in service.

4.5: This carburettor and inlet manifold shows the original TR2 setup. Note the shape of the inlet manifold and the two-stud fixings holding each carburettor in place.

Fuel is fed to the carburettors, which, on the TR2 should be twin 1½in H4 SUs, and twin 1¾in H6 SUs on the TR3/3A/3B/. Both types are fed by an AC model EU mechanical fuel pump located on the nearside of the engine, and driven off the camshaft.

1 Fuel tank and filler

There are two types of fuel tank used by the sidescreen TRs. Both are pressed steel affairs, with a central filler neck, and sit under the rear tonneau panel; but that's where the similarities end. The first type of fuel tank is recognisable by having a 'stepped' bottom in order to fit the contours of the body floor. After TS60001, when the rear body floor pressing was redesigned, there was no need for this step on the fuel tank, but even so fuel capacity was reduced to 11¾ gallons from the original 12.5 gallons (Imperial) of the TR2.

With a typical fuel consumption of 25-30mpg it gave the sidescreen TRs a usable range of up to 330+ miles. The author regularly used to get 40mpg out of his TR2, and, in 1957, one TR2 owner recorded an amazing 71mpg over the 600-mile Mobilgas Economy Run!

The works Le Mans cars featured much larger, long-range tanks to reduce the need for refuelling stops, and there are some aftermarket reproduction tanks available that can offer up to 14 gallons/64 litres capacity, giving a theoretical range of over 400 miles (very useful when touring but that extra three gallons does add another 30lb of weight to the car).

The fuel gauge sender is located in the top face of the tank, and is generally a very reliable unit. Floats have been known to spring a leak, however, but it is a straightforward job to replace the sender unit. The fuel gauge itself is also very reliable in service, but it is unwise to allow the fuel in the tank to fall to near empty.

4.6: The earlier type of 'stepped' steel fuel tank.

4.7: The later type of fuel tank as fitted from TS60001. This is an aluminium reproduction tank, so the steel securing straps need to be isolated from it to prevent electrolytic corrosion.

4.8: The fuel tank sender unit and float.

Despite the presence of in-line filters, dirt, debris and rust can build up in a tank and cause blockages to the system. This is especially so with the early 'stepped' type tank, which does seem more prone to rusting than the later type. Better to keep the tank topped up if possible, but if you're keeping the car in storage for long periods of time then it's better to drain the system, as the fuel will lose its volatility over time, and will also invite water contamination from condensation.

However, steel tanks also suffer from internal corrosion, because petrol/gasoline always has some water contamination in it, and an empty tank can also be exposed to water vapour. Usually the corrosion isn't serious, but sediment and flaking can build up in the tank and clog the outlets. There are a number of tank sealant products on the market, but if the tank is showing signs of corrosion it is better to replace it. If that's the case, then it's time to consider fitting an aluminium tank instead. They're not cheap, at around £350, but it's generally a fit and forget option.

The fuel tanks have a separate vent pipe via a banjo connection attached at the top of the tank on the right-hand side. This vents out through the boot floor. Fuel filler caps on later models of TRs also have a vent, and it's quite possible to fit one of these if yours has corroded too much to re-chrome.

SU carburettors and inlet manifolds

The TR2 used two-bolt fixing 1½in H4 SU carburettors, as shown in fig 4.3, whereas the TR3/3A and 3Bs used 1¾in H6 SU carburettors on the 'square' inlet manifold with four-stud fixings, as shown in fig 4.9. Both of these carburettors were fitted with brass dashpot dampers.

The carburettors and inlet manifolds on many early cars have since been swapped for the more efficient 'Y'-shaped design of inlet manifold, as fitted to the later TR4 model (see Fig 4.10).

Both types of SU carburettor are very reliable in normal service. A needle valve allows fuel to enter the carburettor where it is mixed with air before passing into the engine via the manifold.

Carburettor needles come in various profiles. The official workshop manual states that TR2s used TD needles while early TR3s used TE needles, but these were

4.9: Twin 1¾in H6 SUs as fitted to a high-port head TR3A. Note the wire mesh air filters. The pipe clips on the fuel lines are a sensible but later addition, as they were never fitted by the factory.

both superseded by SM needles at engine No TS10037E. Meanwhile, Burlen Fuel Systems and Bill Piggott, both experts in their field, state that TR2s used FV, CR and GE/R needles, and TR3s used SM, SL and RH needles. Having spoken to both Burlen and Bill Piggott about this anomaly one is left wondering who is right? It's known that the SU part numbers supplied to Triumph were AUC721 (TR2) and AU3786 (TR3).

If the carburettors are from a restoration project then it's probably a good idea to strip them down completely. When SU ceased trading, Burlen Fuel Services bought up stocks of SU parts, and can now recondition almost any type of carburettor. The parts that wear most are the throttle spindles, the bushes and the throttle disc itself. Dashpot and throttle return springs can all be replaced, and the whole carburettor will benefit from a through degreasing and cleaning before reassembly.

Finally, the fuel feed lines on the TR2 and TR3 models should lead to brass 'banjo' style fittings. On the later TR3A/3B models, penny pinching by Triumph meant that these banjo fittings were replaced with cheaper 'push-on' rubberised piping.

The wire mesh air filters, which were a

4.11: Original wire mesh air filters and the 1½in H4 SU carburettors.

4.10: This pair of HS6 SU carburettors has been fitted to the better but later TR4 'Y'-shaped manifold. It's a popular modification for owners of early cars.

4.12: One of the articulated ball joints on the throttle mechanism (circled). See also fig 4.13.

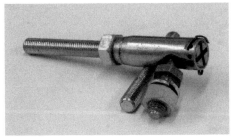

4.13: A close-up of the articulated throttle ball joint. Note the cotter pin has been peened over to hold the crossheaded screw adjuster in place.

feature of all the early TRs, have often been replaced these days with the later TR4 pancake-style air filters. Wire mesh filters, as shown in figure 4.11, should be removed every so often and given a through cleaning with paraffin to remove any road dirt.

One thing that is often overlooked is the condition of the throttle linkages. The author has experienced at firsthand what can happen if one of the ball sockets connecting the throttle drops out while travelling. Trust me, it's not good!

Fuel filter and pump

Located on the left-hand side and towards the rear of the engine, the fuel pump is a combined unit with the fuel filter. All too often this easily accessible unit can get neglected. The fuel pump is driven by a cam drive on the camshaft, and servicing this pump and filter is quite straightforward.

A thumb screw below the glass sight bowl allows for it to be removed and for any sediment that has built up to be cleaned away. Care needs to be taken when removing, cleaning and replacing the cork gasket and gauze filter.

By undoing the set screws in the top of the pump you can gain access to the pump diaphragm. This is the one part that can cause trouble, as a split diaphragm won't allow fuel to get

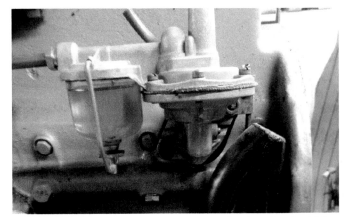

4.14: The AC mechanical fuel pump. Note the glass bowl, which should be checked for signs of water or sediment.

to the carburettors. It's a straightforward task to replace this, but in 40-plus years of TR motoring the author has only had to do this job once. Being a mechanical pump there is also a manual priming lever, which is really useful when starting an engine after a long period of idleness. It is also a good idea to check for water contamination if

4.15: The rubber diaphragm that sits inside the fuel filter housing.

the car has been left standing for long periods without being regularly turned over.

The inlet manifold
As indicated earlier, two types of manifold are used on the sidescreen cars. The early 'square' two-stud type and the later four-stud type. Later cars also had provision for emissions control and servo take-offs. As both types of inlet manifold are a one-piece alloy casting very little can go wrong. If the engine does seem to be running rough, though, check that fuel is being delivered to the inlet manifold correctly. An air leak would be the most likely culprit.

Modifications
By virtue of having largely identical engines, the performance of both the TR2 and the TR3 series can be improved by fitting better manifolds and carburettors.

Some owners have opted to fit purpose-made tubular steel exhaust manifolds, while others have 'upgraded' their older 'square' inlet manifolds for the later 'Y' type, which improves airflow into the combustion chamber.

If performance is your goal then it's possible to fit larger, 2in SU carburettors, which will fit straight on to a four-stud manifold. Alternatively, you may wish to fit twin-choke Weber carburettors, in either 40, 42 or 45mm sizes, but these will also require a change of inlet manifold for them to fit.

Having fitted Weber carburettors, it's worthwhile considering converting the mechanical fuel pump to an electric one. This is especially true if you're contemplating competition work, as the mechanical feed might not be up to the job.

Adding an electric fuel pump is a fairly straightforward conversion, with perhaps where best to site the new pump the

4.16: Twin Weber 45s on this TR3 not only increase power but also fuel consumption!

4.17: The twin electric fuel pumps installed in the boot of the author's TR3S.

biggest consideration. As can be seen in figure 4.17, the author opted to fit two electric pumps to his race car, close to the fuel tank. However, on a road car a single electric pump under the bonnet would be just as good.

Finally, why not pay some attention to the filler cap on the tank. The standard fitment is a spring-loaded chrome cap, which could flip open in the event of an accident. While a number of locking petrol caps were available in period, a better and more attractive solution is to fit a Le Mans style cap, which still has a quick release mechanism but has the added advantage of having a locking insert to stop your tank being siphoned by some miscreant.

4.18: A Le Mans-style fuel cap with a locking insert.

5 The ignition system

5.1: A distributor on a TR3A. Note the absence of a vacuum advance mechanism.

The TR2 was fitted with a Lucas ignition system. This comprised a standard HT coil, a type DM2 distributor fitted with contact breaker points (later changed to a DM2-P4 unit on the TR3A), and a 'self healing' capacitor. It also has a built-in vacuum timing control, the vacuum being taken directly from the inlet manifold. The distributor is driven by a skew gear operated by the camshaft. An Identification number is stamped onto the distributor body, and this should be checked as it's not unknown for an engine to be have been rebuilt using the wrong type of distributor.

Common problems

Wear is probably the biggest problem facing the owner today. It's hard to see and can be difficult to trace. Both the low tension (LT) and high tension (HT) sides of the ignition circuitry can cause problems, which usually manifest themselves when trying to start the car, but they can also bring a car to an unexpected halt with no immediately visible signs of a cause. Wear is also compounded by the dubious quality of some re-manufactured parts, especially some rotor arms and distributor caps, which have been known to fail in operation. Finally, check the condition of ALL the wiring. Very often a fault can be traced to a cracked or broken wire in the HT or LT circuits, and it's much cheaper to replace a set of plug leads than to have a distributor rebuilt.

The distributor

Although a relatively small part of a TR's mechanicals, the distributor is one of the most important components of the engine, and it needs to be looked after.

High mileage cars will suffer from wear on the main distributor driveshaft and its bearings. If you feel any lateral play in the shaft, a specialist rebuild will be required. Play here means the car will suffer from an inconsistent contact breaker gap and dwell angle, and this makes setting the points accurately impossible. Fluctuations in voltage and ignition timing may also be experienced.

5.2: Removing the cap from the same TR3A's distributor shows it to be an electronic one. Note the absence of any points.

5.3: Looking inside a standard distributor. The base plate, condenser and points can be clearly seen. The rotor arm has been removed for clarity.

The distributor cap can also suffer hairline cracks, and both the central spring-loaded HT carbon contact and the individual plug lead contacts can show signs of wear. If in doubt, replace it, especially if your TR is difficult to start during damp weather.

Other key parts located inside the distributor are the capacitor, the base plate, the rotor arm, and, of course, the contact breaker points. Points should be checked for wear and be re-gapped every 5000 miles. The base plate can also become loose and move inside the distributor, which will make it very difficult to adjust the points.

Points can burn out, and, if they have, should be replaced. The pivot and cam bearing should be lubricated with a drop of thin machine oil at the same time as the cam on the distributor shaft is given a small amount of grease: but DO NOT get oil or grease on or near the contacts.

The author has fitted an electronic distributor to one of his TRs, but he has found very little difference between the two

5.4: Inside another distributor fitted with an advance/retard mechanism. This time there is a rotor arm but no condenser or points; the black box marks out this distributor as a contactless one. There is obviously a lot less to go wrong!

systems in everyday running. However, he still carries a spare base plate and a set of points in his travelling tool kit.

3 The sparkplugs

When having trouble starting an engine one of the first things to check is the condition of the sparkplugs. Dirty, oil- or petrol-soaked plugs will impede starting, so make sure they are clean, dry, and properly gapped at 0.025in (the normal gap). Also check the white insulator on the plugs for cracks.

When checking the plugs make sure the number printed on them matches that in the handbook. Champion LS10 sparkplugs were used initially, and LS11 for high speed running with a gap of 0.032 thou (0.8mm). However, Bosch W9AC are also a suitable sparkplug for normal road use. The author often uses Champion N-9Y sparkplugs, but there are other compatible sparkplugs from the likes of NGK and Lodge. If non-standard plugs are being used, it may be the case that the engine has been modified in some way in order to require 'colder' plugs.

The colour of the electrodes is a good indicator of the health of the engine. Every plug should be the same (grey) colour, but

5.5: Check you have the right sparkplug, and that it's correctly gapped.

if not, and one or two are significantly different, this indicates combustion chamber wear. Replace the plugs with new ones, and, if the plugs continue to look different to each other, further diagnosis will be required to find the cause of the problem, possibly compression loss or piston ring wear. Incidentally, sparkplugs have a normal efficient life of approximately 10,000 miles, after which they should be replaced rather than cleaned.

When removing or fitting sparkplugs it's best to use a proper plug socket with a rubber insert in it to protect the ceramic part of the plug. However, a carefully used box spanner will also do the job. A smear of graphite grease on the threads is also a good idea, to prevent plugs seizing up and damaging the head. There is a ring gasket fitted on each plug, which is often overlooked, but its function is to seal in the cylinder gases. A broken ring gasket will affect the running of the engine. Finally, sparkplugs need to be firmly tightened, but not so hard as to strip the thread!

4 The coil

The coil forms part of the high tension (HT) circuit and is bolted to the side of the engine. Consequently, they can and do get very hot, and this can cause them to fail. Some owners prefer to

5.6: This TR3 has been fitted with an uprated 'Gold' sports coil ... a highly recommended option.

5.7: Competition TRs often have a second coil fitted to the inner wing, but it's also a good place to carry a spare coil.

relocate the coil away from the engine block onto the wheelarch, and carry a spare coil as well.

Other problems can be caused by loose spade connectors or a broken wire due to age, vibration or corrosion. If the engine cuts out when hot the coil itself may be at fault. Let the engine cool down and if it restarts then it's almost certain that the coil is faulty. Replace it with a 'Gold' sports coil if possible, as shown in Fig 5.6, or carry a spare coil as shown in Fig 5.7.

5 Electronic ignition (EI) or EMS
Often viewed as a 'magic cure' for old ignition systems, fitting a solid state electronic ignition has become a very popular

modification because of its 'fit and forget' advertising slogans. EI is undoubtedly very reliable and performs well under most conditions.

Early systems required a separate black box to be mounted externally to the engine, but today it's possible to have an EI distributor fitted and keep the engine bay looking completely original.

Having a fully mapped engine management system for a TR is not a cheap option. A basic electronic distributor can be had for about £400, but you can pay anything between £800 and £1500 for a fully programmable EI system. If you add on the price of throttle bodies and all that goes with it you can easily spend £7000 or more, so if you only do a few thousand miles per year you really have to consider if it's worth fitting. On the plus side, with legislation getter tougher all the time, it should keep your car's emissions in check.

Starting problems
Poor starting can be traced to a number of problems, but after eliminating the obvious one of having no fuel then the next thing to do is to check for a spark. Removing a plug lead and shorting it to earth on a rocker cover nut (while turning over the engine) will reveal whether or not there is a spark. If there is a good spark then the problem will probably lie elsewhere. Alternatively, remove a sparkplug and see if there is a good spark there. However, if there is no spark, or only a very weak one, then the problem is likely to be in either the HT or LT circuit. A multimeter check on the ignition circuit should show a reading of 12v on the coil input. If not, check the battery is giving the required 12 volts. Often when cars have been left standing over the winter the battery is one of the first things to go wrong. Using a low voltage trickle charger can help prevent this.

Next, remove the distributor cap and check for a spark at the points, and that the contacts are in good condition. Again, if there's no spark then it might be a broken wire on the LT side of the distributor. Also check the distributor and rotor arm for cracks and wear. Finally, don't forget to check all of the HT leads – including the lead from the coil to the distributor – as they can deteriorate over time.

Running-on problems

If the engine continues to run for a short time after the ignition has been turned off, there is most likely a problem with the fuel/air mixture causing the fuel vapour to be ignited due to excessive heat in the combustion chamber rather than by the sparkplug itself.

Possible causes for this are over advanced ignition timing, too high an idling speed (it should be 750-800rpm and not 1000rpm), a very high compression ratio, incorrect sparkplugs, or an excess of carbon build up in the combustion chamber creating hot spots. If none of these are present then it may be necessary to fit an aftermarket anti-run-on valve that would allow more air to enter the engine.

If you rule out all of the above checks then another possibility could be an electrical 'surge' in the ignition circuit. This can happen if an aftermarket electrical accessory, like a Kenlowe fan, for example, has been fitted. Aftermarket accessories have been known to cause running-on problems if they've been wired directly into the ignition circuit. Fitting a relay to that circuit should prevent this happening. However, if the problem still persists

5.8: Visibly damaged teeth on the camshaft drive gear, possibly caused by poor lubrication or an ill-fitting distributor drive.

after fitting a relay try turning on the wipers. If the engine cuts out immediately it will confirm the electrical problem, as turning the wipers on will 'drain' power from the ignition circuit.

Finally, one should remember that the ignition system is driven by the camshaft acting on a skew gear on the distributor shaft. These gears can and do wear, as photo 5.8 shows. No amount of adjustment will enable the engine to run correctly if these gears are damaged, and the only option is to tear down the engine and replace the damaged parts.

6 The cooling system

The distinct 'mouth' on the TR2/3's front apron greatly helped to direct air through the radiator. On the later 'wide mouth' TR3A, however, fibreboard panels had to be added to help duct airflow toward the radiator. All models use a vertical flow radiator fitted with a 3.5-4.5lb release pressure cap as standard. However, many cars now use higher-rated pressure caps with seemingly no ill effects: a $7lb/in^2$ pressure cap being not uncommon.

A 12.5in four-blade engine-driven fan mounted on the crankshaft pulley provides a cooling draught through the radiator.

A notable feature of the TR2/3/3A/3B radiator was the long filler neck that doubles as a header tank. This was necessitated by the position of the radiator being placed well forward under the front apron. These radiators all have a starting handle hole in their cores, which somewhat reduces the cooling properties. Some owners have forgone this starting handle hole when repairing their cars, and have fitted the later TR4 type cores, as these offer slightly better cooling.

The system itself can be drained by removing the radiator filler cap, opening the heater control valve on the cylinder head, and opening the drain taps situated at the bottom of the radiator and on the right-hand side of the engine block.

The thermostat

The thermostat housing situated at the front of the engine controls the operating temperature, and water is circulated by a four-vane belt-driven water pump.

The first 1200 TR2s had what are known as a double

6.1: The standard metal fan has been known to lose blades due to metal fatigue, so it's worth checking blade condition.

6.2: An alloy radiator is an expensive upgrade, but can provide up to 40% better cooling than the standard item.

6.3: The rare double thermostat housing as fitted to the first TR2s has been remade, thanks to the TR Spares Development Fund.

thermostat housing. This apparently proved troublesome in service, and was soon replaced by the more common single thermostat housing found on most cars. The original twin thermostat housing is a rare sight these days on a TR2. However, the TRSDF has recently commissioned a new batch to be made for those seeking originality.

Thermostats should be set to open at 1580 F/700C, and the reading on the temperature gauge during normal motoring should not exceed 1850F/850C. If it does then there is problem!

1 Coolant leaks

Any loss of coolant should be immediately apparent from the temperature gauge, and should be investigated straight away. Leaks from hoses or the radiator itself should be easy to spot. Less obvious are leaks from core plugs in the block, of which there are several, or from the heater. The water pump can also give problems if the bearing starts to fail. Rusty coolant water stains are often the best tell-tale way to trace a leak, and for the most part rectification is a straightforward replacement of the affected parts.

However, if white smoke is seen coming from the exhaust, and the coolant constantly needs topping up, then head gasket failure is the most likely cause. Poor running will also be evident.

2 Overheating

The temperature gauge should be holding at a steady 1850°F /850°C, but when going up long hills it's quite normal for the needle to climb to 1940°F/900°C or even more, but it should quickly return to normal soon afterwards. If, however, it persists in reading higher temperatures, that indicates a cooling system deficiency. This may be due to poor water circulation, a blocked radiator, a sticking thermostat, low coolant level, or the aforementioned cylinder head gasket failure.

Under normal driving conditions most cars never need a fan as enough air is pushed through the radiator. It's only in town driving or in traffic queues that the fan comes into its own. Many owners dispense with the original metal fan and fit an electric one instead, complete with a manual override in the cockpit. If you go down this route, remember that the metal fan, which was mounted on rubber bushes, also acted as a crankshaft balancer, so a new crank balancer will need to be fitted to ensure dynamic stability. Failure to do so can lead to the crank breaking in two!

It's also important to not only fit the correct fan but to make sure it's the right way round! Experience says its best to fit a new fan behind and as close to the radiator as possible, rather than if front of it (see Fig 6.2). A fan mounted on the front of the radiator blocks off quite a lot of the radiator core, and it will require a 'pusher' type fan blade to be fitted.

After many miles on the road the radiator can become blocked with debris and insects. The best way to cure this is to remove the radiator and use a high pressure hose to clean it.

Another source of overheating can be from inside the engine block itself. Over the years the build up of sediment in the water jacket of the iron block can severely restrict water flow around the engine. The author has even found casting sand still in situ when undertaking an engine rebuild. Sediment can be removed with proprietary flushing compounds, but it might even be necessary to

6.4: The twin spot lights on the works Le Mans cars didn't cause overheating problems, but then they were doing 90mph for most of the time! On a road car in traffic, on the other hand, overheating could be a problem.

take out the core plugs to remove all the deposits. Finally, owners should be aware that any rally plate, spot lights or badges fixed in front of the grille can also decrease cooling.

3 Over-cooling

It's rare to find a car that is reading over-cooled, or fails to reach normal operating temperature, but it can happen. Usually it's nothing more than a broken sender unit from the thermostat housing, but it might also be the gauge itself which is at fault. If an electric fan is fitted, then that, too, might be the culprit if it's turning on too early, or more likely not turning off! Finally, on an old engine – and all TR2-3Bs are now 'old,' the alloy thermostat housing itself might be suffering from internal corrosion and causing the thermostat to jam. Replace it if necessary.

6.5: Old and new thermostats. The one on the left is shown in the open position.

6.6: The more common form of thermostat housing.

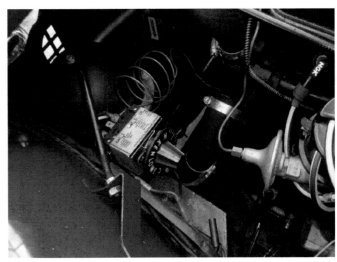

6.7: A Kenlow fan thermostat switch. Note the coiled copper wire to absorb vibration from the engine.

4 The water pump

There are three main parts to the water pump assembly: the cast iron housing that feeds water into the engine block and has the outlet connection to the bottom radiator hose; the water pump itself with the four-vane impeller, and the steel drive pulley. By and large, TR2-3A water pumps are reliable, but, if the drivebelt is over-tightened, it can place unacceptable extra strain on the pump's bearing, causing it to fail. Genuine early TR2-3A water pumps can be greased via a built-in grease nipple, but modern repro units are sealed for life. Another failure that can happen is for the woodruff key to come loose. This key holds the pulley in place on the pump shaft, but excessive wear in its

6.8: The water pump (on the left) and its housing (on the right). This housing is an alloy reproduction unit with a thin-belt alloy pulley in the centre.

locating groove can cause it to slip and eventually fail completely. If the pump needs to be replaced, then it's a case of removing the fanbelt, undoing the three locating bolts on the water pump, taking care over the lower one as it can be difficult to get a spanner on, and removing it from the engine.

At this stage you might want to replace the iron water pump housing with a new alloy one. It's also advisable to fit a new water pump with an uprated impeller with six vanes rather than the usual four, which will improve water circulation through the engine.

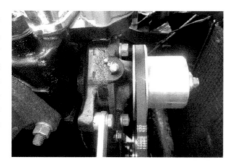

6.9: The owner of this TR has converted the water pump to a thin-belt drive and fitted an alternator at the same time. Note the grease nipple on the water pump itself, and the alloy pulley.

Many owners now convert their cars to run a 'thin-belt' drive instead of the standard 'wide-belt.' This is often carried out when installing an alternator to replace the old dynamo. The crank pulley and fan extension are also removed. The new crank pulley should have a dynamic balancer built into it. A new electric fan replaces the old metal fan. If funds allow this would be a good time to replace the standard radiator with an alloy one.

5 Coolant

Until the advent of waterless cooling products, tap water with antifreeze added was the obvious choice for all motorists. The author has tried waterless cooling in both road and racing cars, but has since reverted back to using the ordinary water/antifreeze solution. Since water boils at 100 degrees C (which is plenty hot enough) any problem with the car's cooling system will soon become apparent, whereas with the waterless system any problems with the engine may take longer to detect. This is not to say that waterless cooling is to be avoided, but it's an expensive replacement for an already well proven system for cooling a car engine. If sticking to the more traditional mix of water and antifreeze, make sure you get the balance right. Having too much antifreeze can be as bad as having too little. In any case the whole system should be flushed out every three years, ideally just in time for the winter, and filled with new antifreeze.

6 The heater

An often overlooked part of the car's cooling system is the heater. Although it was originally listed as an optional extra, the majority of cars sold in the UK were fitted with one. The heater system only adds another pint of water to the cooling system, but it uses the same water that circulates around the engine, so it also needs to be kept in good shape. The standard Smiths heater (model number CHS 920/4) was probably only just adequate when the cars were new. I say just about adequate since anyone who expects it to be on a par with modern air-conditioning will be in for a big shock! Poor heating performance can be attributed to:

1. A faulty thermostat preventing the right coolant temperature being reached.
2. The electric blower motor might be inoperative, probably due to the switch being defective.
3. An air lock in the water system.
4. The heater valve on the engine not being turned on fully or stuck in the closed position.
5. A blocked heater matrix.

The last item is basically a very small radiator, which acts as the heat exchanger and so can suffer from the same faults as the full-sized radiator. Leaks in the heater matrix are often first revealed by the discovery of wet carpets!

6.11: A Clayton heater from Revington TR as fitted in this LHD TR.

The two rubber pipes passing through the bulkhead to the heater are also often overlooked. Those located under the bulkhead are out of sight, but age can harden and crack them. The same applies to those in the engine bay, but a close visual inspection here will give an indication of what the internal pipes might be like.

If undertaking a full rebuild it can be advisable to fit an uprated heater from one of the aftermarket suppliers. Revington TR offers a very good alternative 4kW two-speed Clayton heater, which fits neatly into the same space occupied by the Smiths unit.

The heater valve on an early TR is a pretty basic bit of plumbing, being a screw down valve just like a domestic water stopcock (see Fig 6.9). It's possible to fit a later TR4 type valve or an aftermarket slide-type heater valve, but that will require a push-pull mounting plinth to be fixed somewhere inside the cockpit.

6.10: The original Smiths heater.

6.12: The green control wheel on this standard TR2/3 heater valve can only be operated from under the bonnet.

7 Steering & front suspension

The front suspension and steering on a TR are what we might describe as being rugged in their design. Although somewhat crude by today's standards, nevertheless the setup was effective and had few faults other than being rather heavy. There was no servo assistance, and, while rack and pinion steering would have made a real difference, this would not appear on a TR until the introduction of the TR4.

The steering
The cars are fitted with a proprietary cam and lever type of steering box made by Alford and Alder. These are now very difficult to source, but by the 1970s wear in the steering box was already a common cause of MOT failure. The drop arm on the steering box connects to the various tie rods that articulate the steering. The outer

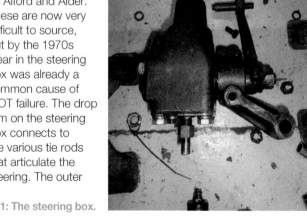

7.1: The steering box.

steering column is a hefty bit of tubing passing right through the bulkhead. The inner column, which is connected to the steering wheel, works the steering box, and also acts as a housing for the wiring to the horn and indicators. Later, a two-piece steering column was introduced, which was adjustable for length.

The steering assembly
The steering assembly is a very reliable unit, the only real wear and tear being found in the four tie rod ends, which occasionally need replacing. The tie rod ends can (should) be fitted with grease nipples, and should be regularly checked for wear (get an assistant to waggle the steering wheel while you feel for movement in the ball joints). Tie rod end wear can make itself evident by sloppy steering, uneven tyre wear, and clunking noises.

Steering alignment
Maintaining the correct castor and camber angles is important, but modern laser tracking devices very often do not measure these. As these cars have a proper chassis it is possible that any previous accident damage has twisted the chassis out of true. Only a proper drop check can verify this, but if the steering on the car continues to feel vague after replacing worn out parts then this should be considered and undertaken by a specialist.

The front suspension
Some common problems
The suspension on any car has to do a lot of very hard work,

7.2: The front suspension and steering box mounting.

of this setup is wear on the trunnion and kingpin assembly due to a lack of lubrication, and this will be dealt with in greater detail below. Woolly steering is caused by excessive play in the steering geometry, and any 'clunks' from the front suspension need to be investigated immediately as they can be signs of wear in bushes.

1 The top wishbone

The top wishbone design is easily identified by its angular square-section profile and the single-bolt top ball joint fixing. The wishbone is formed by two steel pressings that fit on to the upper fulcrum pin. This is a separate forging held in place by four bolts on top of the spring tower. Two part 'top-hat' style rubber bushes are used here, and are prone to wear. Meanwhile, the outer ends of the wishbones take the universal ball joint, which fits into the top of the king pin. A distance piece is used in the pressings in order to help locate the ball joint. Just one nut is used to secure it.

New split pins should be used on the castellated nuts on the fulcrum pins, and, finally, a grease nipple should be fitted to this top ball joint to aid lubrication if one isn't already present.

so it's important to keep it in good working order. The front suspension on a TR2-3B is of the double wishbone type, and can easily be maintained by any competent home mechanic. The Achilles heel

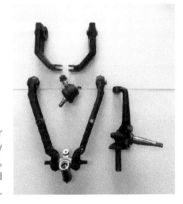

7.3: The original style upper and lower wishbone assembly together with the top ball joint, the king pin/vertical link, and the bronze trunnion.

7.4: These later style TR4 top wishbones fitted to a TR3 show how the arms are now handed. The front of the car is to the right.

2 King pin (vertical link) and stub axle assembly

This is one of the most critical parts of the front suspension, and probably where you'll find most of the wear in the system. The king pin, or vertical link as it's sometimes known, is a single forging with three distinct areas to it. Firstly, there is the hole in the top that takes the upper universal joint for the top wishbones. Then there is the stub axle itself, which passes through the king pin. And finally there's the lower threaded part, which screws into the bronze trunnion. It is this lower threaded bit that can suffer from most of the wear associated with king pins. Wear on this part can be very rapid and the damaged thread can sometimes be seen to be 'waisted' along its length. The author's own race car suffered from 'waisting' after doing less than 3000 miles. The stub axle itself is usually trouble-free, but if the wheel bearings get damaged or badly worn then scoring of the shaft can occur. They can also get bent from accident damage so do check them.

New, larger diameter and stronger stub axles can be bought, but they require new front hubs to be fitted as well. The stub axle is mounted on

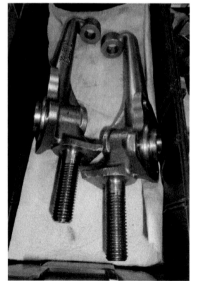

7.5: The vertical links or king pins.

7.6: The front suspension assembly stripped down. Note the grease nipple in the bronze trunnion and the tapered stub axle bearing shaft.

the vertical link or king pin and it is this that carries the front hub and wheel bearing assembly.

3 The lower wishbone, fulcrum pin and trunnion

The lower wishbones are located on bushes to the fulcrum brackets, and these are mounted on the chassis either side of the spring towers. The lower wishbones also hold the spring pan in place. The U-shaped brackets have shims behind them, and it's by adding or removing shims that the suspension geometry can be altered. The outer ends of hold the trunnion in place, which, in turn, houses the king pin.

The trunnions are bronze castings, available with varying degrees of inclination, and it's important to make sure you get the correct ones for your car. Originally, the trunnions were fitted with a grease nipple at the lower end, but not all cars have these; a sure sign they have been replaced at some time. The same is true for the trackrod ends and the top ball joint.

When fitting new bronze trunnions one tip is to apply some solder around the steel base plate where the grease nipple goes. This will seal it to the trunnion and stop the grease, which is required to lubricate the thread on the vertical link, being lost.

A steel pivot bolt or pin passes right through the trunnion, and it's to this pin that the outer ends of the wishbones are affixed. There are a number of tubular steel bushes, and steel and nylon washers to be fitted onto the pivot bolt, so care must be taken when assembling it. Rubber 'O' rings should also be fitted to protect these bushes from dirt. With the car

7.8: This is one of the bronze trunnions that can wear badly if not kept well greased. The steel cross pin can also suffer from wear.

safely jacked up, any play in the suspension setup can be felt by rocking the front wheels in-and-out, top-to-bottom. Any excess movement will be easily felt and needs to be investigated as a matter of urgency.

4 The coil springs

You would think that there isn't very much that can go wrong with a coil spring, and by and large this is true. They have been known to break, though, usually after hitting a large pothole at speed. When that happens the affected corner will sag and steering will become difficult, if not impossible. When rebuilding a TR, it is important to get not only the right length of spring but also one of the correct rate. Springs can sometimes have different colour paint on them (red, yellow and blue, for example), which usually indicates different spring rates. The springs should be fitted with rubber rings to prevent noise and chafing with the lower spring pan and the top mounting. Alloy spacer blocks of different thicknesses can also be placed above the spring to get the correct ride height. Always replace both springs at the same time.

Stripping the front suspension is a straightforward affair that can be undertaken by any competent home mechanic, but my advice is to borrow or hire a spring compressor of the type that passes *inside* the coil spring rather than those that clamp externally onto the coils.

5 The shock absorbers

Oil-filled telescopic shock absorbers are fitted to the front suspension, and they sit inside the coil springs. Located at the bottom by four bolts to the lower spring pan and a single locking nut at the top of the spring tower, they are very easy to replace with adjustable items, such as those from Koni or Spax.

A general service should check that the securing nuts are still tight and that there are no signs of oil weeping from the units. A quick test to see if they are working properly is to 'bounce' the front wing. If it continues to bounce more than one and a half times then check the shockers and replace if necessary. Always replace shock absorbers and springs in matched pairs. Failure to do so will result in poor handling and extra wear on the system.

6 Bump stops

The humble bump stop plays an important role in making the ride more comfortable. At the bottom of the suspension tower there is large bracket fixed by two long bolts to the chassis. On to this bracket is fixed the bump stop rubber, which sits under the spring pan. It does get a bit neglected so do check on its condition (see Fig 7.9). There are also domed-shaped bump rubbers fitted to the middle of the wishbone arms (see Fig 7.7). Again, do check the condition of these rebound rubbers.

7.9: The lower bump stop bracket and rebound rubber.

7 Front wheel bearings

There are two bearings in each wheel hub, an inner and an outer ball race. As long as the bearings are correctly set up and not over-tightened or too slack they should perform without any trouble. Original equipment bearings were very good, and Timken makes very good bearings, too, but there are a number of very inferior bearings now on the market and the temptation to fit these can be a false economy.

With the car safely jacked up, a spin of the wheel will reveal any rumbles from the bearings if they are showing signs of wear. A further test is to hold the wheel in the 12 o'clock/6 o'clock positions and try rocking it. Any play will show the wheel bearings need either tightening or replacing. Regular greasing is also a must if they are to be maintained properly.

Improvements

For ordinary road car use the standard front suspension setup and steering are fine. An alternative is to fit a rack and pinion conversion kit, of which there are a number on the market. If the TR's heavy steering is still too much for you then it's possible to fit a powered steering rack. These can be electric or hydraulic, but neither is going to be a cheap conversion.

1 Rack and pinion conversion

Converting a TR2/3 to rack and pinion steering is a big undertaking and best left to a specialist. A new two-piece steering column is required, and the original indicator switch may have to be discarded, although the horn push can be kept. The rack can be mounted to the chassis either horizontally or vertically, as the accompanying two photos show.

If competition is contemplated then there are a number of things you can do to improve the handling of the car. First of all, fitting stronger springs and adjustable shock absorbers are a straightforward bolt-on improvement. Secondly, altering the camber angle to give 1.5 degrees of negative camber will improve the handling. This can be done by modifying the top wishbones to make them shorter. Some TR specialists can also offer modified wishbones from stock.

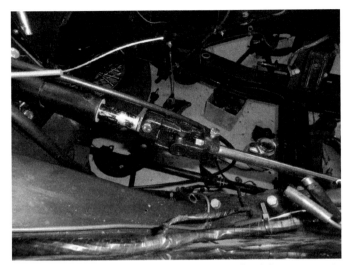

7 10: This rack and pinion conversion has retained the upper part of the steering column, and a new coupling has been fitted.

2 Front anti-roll bar

Anti-roll bars were originally only ever a factory-fitted option on the TR3A/B, but early cars could have one fitted by one of several aftermarket suppliers who supplied bars of different diameters for road or competition use. Diagram 7.13 overleaf shows how the SAH anti-roll bar is fixed to the side of the chassis by brackets, and to the lower front wishbone by articulated drop links. As the rubber fittings can perish over time, some people retro fit spherical rose joints instead.

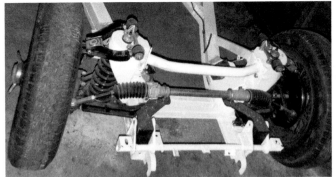

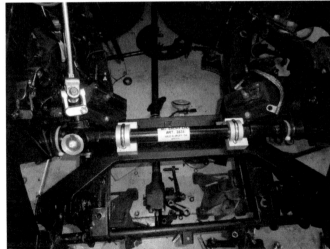

7.11 (top) and 7.12 (above): Two different ways of mounting a steering rack to a TR2/3.

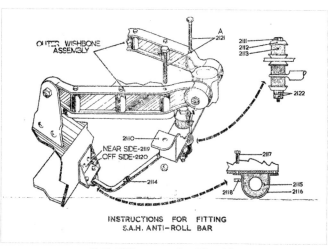

7.13: Fitting an anti-roll bar kit.

7.14: This shows the two-piece square section top wishbone. In the circle is the brass lock stop to prevent the wheel turning too far.

8 Rear suspension

8.1: The rear axle and suspension setup. The alloy diff cover and short Panhard rod are non-standard items.

The springs

The rear suspension of the TR2/3/3A/3B uses a leaf spring setup dictated in part by the use of the live Mayflower back axle. The spring has six semi-elliptical laminated leaves, or blades, as they are sometimes called. The front end of the spring is fixed to the chassis by a substantial steel pin (see Fig 8.2).

This pin can, in theory, be removed for replacement, but if it's badly worn then a great deal of force will be required to remove it

8.2: The spring locating pin.

from the chassis! It once took the author two days of hard work to remove and replace one, so it's definitely not a job for the faint-hearted.

The tail ends of the springs are fixed to the rear of the chassis by floating spring shackles, and are held in place by top-hat rubber bushes. These are much easier to replace.

If you're unfortunate enough to break a leaf in a spring, then changing it is a relatively straightforward job that can be accomplished at home. It will probably

8.3: The rear spring shackle.

encourage much swearing, though, for although the rear end of the spring and its other attachments are easy to unbolt, getting the front end of the spring off the aforementioned steel pin can be a bit of a struggle. On more than one occasion the author has resorted to the oxy-acetylene torch to burn out the bush holding the spring in place when it wouldn't come off. As not every home mechanic has access to such equipment, you may want to enlist the help of a garage to do this work. If the steel shackle pin has become 'waisted' from wear where it passes through the bush, then it, too, must be replaced. As indicated above, this is not a very easy job to do with the car's body in place, but is much easier to do if you are carrying out a full restoration on a stripped or rolling chassis. Using penetrating oil and heat is the key to freeing this pin, as is the use of a press tool. Hitting the end of the pin with a large hammer is unlikely to do much to move it, but it may shock the pin free.

When reassembling the spring it's a good idea to smear the shackle pins with Copaslip™. The factory recommended brushing the sides of the blades with engine oil, which was sufficient to keep them lubricated. Alternatively, the spring itself could be wrapped in oilcloth retained by tie tags, which would stop bits of grit getting in between the leaves and causing irritating squeals as you drive along.

Rear springs are often replaced with stronger, higher rated 'competition' items, but this can be a mistake as the ride quality will suffer. You need to ask yourself what end use will the car have, and, if it's just for touring, then there's nothing wrong with the standard setup.

Shock absorbers

Armstrong lever arm dampers are fitted to brackets on the chassis by two bolts that pass through the shock absorber's body. These bolts have a habit of working loose, so it's best to replace them with longer bolts that can pass through the rear of the brackets. You can then secure these with Nyloc nuts. The dampers can leak oil, so it's worth checking and topping up the fluid from time to time.

8.4: The standard Armstrong lever damper. Note the rubber axle bump stop and the check strap over the axle.

This can be done on later versions of the shock absorber by undoing the small filler plug on the top of the unit. Uprated shock absorbers are available, as are adjustable ones, if you can find them, which have a knurled knob at the bottom (see Fig 8.5).

Even rarer (think hens' teeth!) are the twin-piston dampers, which work on both bump and rebound. A vertical drop link connects the lever arm of the damper to a lug on the base plate of the spring. The rubber bushes in these drop links perish over time and can wear to such an extent that the links can come adrift, with predictably adverse results on the car's handling. It is relatively easy to make

8.5: An adjustable lever arm shock absorber and rear anti-roll bar setup.

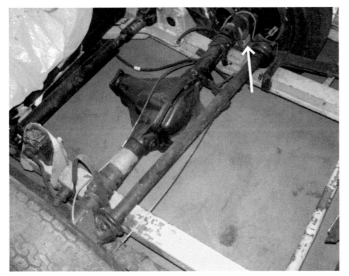

A large U-shaped check strap is also fitted to the chassis to restrict the amount of axle movement, and the axle itself should have bump and rebound rubbers fixed to the axle tube just above the chassis (see Fig 8.4). These rubbers are often missing from cars that have been rebuilt as there doesn't seem to be a way of reattaching them onto the axle tube. However, the way to do this is to cut through one side of the rubber, open it out so it can go round the axle tube and then use locking wire to secure it in place. It's a simple but effective remedy.

Suspension problems

By and large suspension problems on a live axle car are few and far between. As long as the suspension is properly maintained and lubricated it should give many miles of trouble-free motoring. Broken springs need to be replaced in pairs, as do shock absorbers and drop links. To do otherwise is unwise as the ride can be affected. Check the condition of the bushes, and, if excessive movement is detected, replace as necessary.

Modifications

There are a few modifications that

8.6: Another view of the rear suspension. The U-straps over the axle can be clearly seen. Note the alloy spacer block between the spring and the axle at the top of the photo (arrowed). The Panhard rod was a period modification for competition.

8.7: This is a very neat installation on a live axle TR. Note the Alfin-type brake drums and the tie tags securing the bump rubbers to the axle. The U-strap has yet to be fitted.

up a rose jointed version of these drop links, but again, unless competition is your aim, then replacing them with standard units will suffice.

Another key component of the TR's rear suspension that is worth looking at are the alloy spacer blocks that go between the spring and the axle tube casing. These were available, in a variety of sizes, and alter the ride height of the car. The axle is secured to the spring via two large U-bolts that locate the alloy spacer block and pass through to the spring plate below.

can be done to a live axle TR. Although never offered as a factory option, fitting a rear anti-roll bar is one that is favoured by some enthusiasts. On a live axle TR this is accomplished by welding a bracket to the chassis in order to locate the bar, while drop links attach to a modified spring retaining plate. Fig 8.7 shows a very popular setup designed by Neil Revington of Revington TR.

A Panhard rod, shown in Fig 8.6, is another modification that can help to locate the axle, as are anti-tramp bars to stop axle 'wind up' under hard acceleration. Details of all these modifications can be found in the TR Register's *Technicalities* publication, and I am grateful to Ian Cornish for allowing me to publish his drawings here.

If you are ever worried about bending your axle, then Racetorations offers a Girling axle tube brace kit (see fig 8.8). This bolts onto the axle casing at the diff cover, and clamps around the axle tubes. It's unlikely you would ever have to contemplate fitting this onto a road car, but serious race car owners might get some benefit from it.

Finally, a much more difficult, and some would say drastic, modification is to give the rear axle some negative camber. This is definitely not a job you can do in your garage as it requires a great deal of engineering skill to make sure it's done properly. With the axle completely stripped down, the top of the axle tubes have to be heated and then cooled rapidly in order to induce some shrinkage, or bent using a press. The author has seen

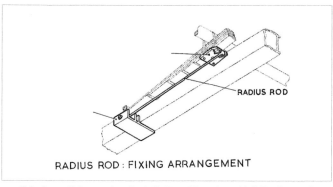

RADIUS ROD : FIXING ARRANGEMENT

8.8: An anti-tramp bar installation. (Courtesy Neil Revington)

8.9: An axle brace for a Girling-type axle, as supplied by Racetorations.

only one example of this being done to a car, but it's said that handling was much improved. Personally, I wouldn't go to such lengths, it's probably easier to buy a fully restored car!

9 Propshaft, axle & rear hubs

The driveline

The TR2, TR3, TR3A and TR3B all shared the same layout of driveline, consisting of a sliding propshaft and a solid-beam axle with a hypoid-bevel semi-floating differential. It's often viewed as old-fashioned and unrefined, but it's a well proven and robust system, which is still common to many cars even today.

Common problems

1 Oil leaks and final drive noise

Oil leaks in the driveline can only come from a single source: the differential case. The differential gears can also be a source of noise (these areas will be addressed later).

2 The propeller shaft

The propeller shaft is a two-piece sliding joint affair that benefits from being regularly lubricated with grease. The sliding joint is a necessity on the TR2-3B as it takes up any movement of the live axle.

The shaft is fitted at both ends with universal joint couplings, and it is advisable to fit joints that can be greased. Wear in the U/J can cause the propshaft to rumble and vibrate. A 'clunk' can often be heard when pulling away from rest or when changing gear when U/Js are worn, but in the worst case the U/Js can break up and cause the propshaft to flail the tunnel with a somewhat alarming noise!

Care should be taken when changing a U/J, as it's quite possible for one of the needle roller bearings to fall out of position and lie unnoticed in the bearing cup. A dab of grease should prevent this from happening, but if you find that you can't easily press the U/J in place, this is the likely cause.

Whilst it's easier to remove the propshaft and replace the U/Js when taking the gearbox out, it can be done from underneath the car as there are only four bolts at each end of the shaft. Care should be taken to replace the bolts the correct way round, though, and to use nyloc nuts (see Fig 9.2).

9.1: The sliding joint on the propeller shaft. Note the grease nipple and the circlip retaining the U/J spider.

9.2: The propshaft coupling. The bolts securing it must pass through the flange so that the nyloc nuts are on the gearbox side. Note the grease nipple, circled.

3 The live axle

While the TR2 and the early TR3s were fitted with Lockheed-type axles based on the Mayflower's design, the later TR3s and all of the TR3As and TR3Bs were fitted with the much stronger Girling axle derived from the Standard Vanguard. While the differentials, axles and axle tubes are the same in both, the half shafts and hub bearings are much stronger on the Girling axle. The Lockheed axle developed a reputation for breaking half shafts under hard or competitive driving, and the ball bearing hubs could also suffer. The introduction of the Girling axle featured taper roller bearings, much stronger half shafts, and a thrust block to the differential pin. The axles are easily distinguished from each other by the number of bolts that secure the brake hub to the axle flange. Lockheed axles have four bolts on a square flange, whereas the Girling axles have a round flange with six bolts.

Both axle arrangements were fitted with a 3.7: 1 final drive ratio on both overdrive and non-overdrive cars. Later, a 4.1:1 ratio was made available during the TR3's production run, but it was only ever an option and not fitted as standard. Even lower ratios are available, but these would probably only be used for competition work.

A serial number can be found stamped on top of the axle casing. Oil capacity is 1.5 pints or 0.8 litres, and this can be topped up after removing the filler plug in the pressed steel rear cover of the differential housing.

Removing a live axle from a car is a lengthy process. It involves jacking up the car and taking off the wheels, remembering to place axle stands under the chassis where the body mounting points are. Next, disconnect the axle from the propshaft and drain the brake fluid from the system. It's then a case of removing the handbrake linkage (see Figs 9.3 and 9.4), the hubs, axle shafts, drum brake assemblies, and the two axle check straps. At this stage the axle is still attached to the car's leaf springs, so these must also be jacked up to take the load off them while the bolts holding the spring plates can be released (to be left hanging on the damper links). However, if you're going this far, you might

9.3: A live axle. The rear disc brakes are non-standard.

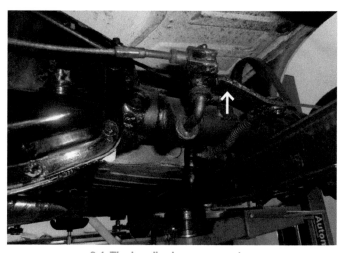

9.4: The handbrake compensator.

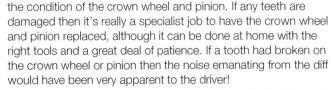

9.5: This is a Girling axle showing the cross pin in the differential cage. If the teeth on the crown wheel show signs of wear, it needs replacing.

as well remove the dampers as well, and give them a good clean.

With the axle now free it's time to remove it. This is best achieved by sliding the axle to the left-hand side of the chassis, so that the right-hand end of the axle tube is clear of the right-hand side of the chassis. It can then be lowered and drawn clear of the car. Having an assistant makes this job so much easier. Refitting the axle is simply the reverse of the above steps.

Once the axle is on the bench it's then a case of inspecting it and deciding what you want to do. Removal of the rear cover will allow you to inspect

9.6: A crown wheel and pinion set. Note the roller bearing cage.

the condition of the crown wheel and pinion. If any teeth are damaged then it's really a specialist job to have the crown wheel and pinion replaced, although it can be done at home with the right tools and a great deal of patience. If a tooth had broken on the crown wheel or pinion then the noise emanating from the diff would have been very apparent to the driver!

With the axle out of the car it is advisable to give it a thorough clean, and to replace all of the oil seals and bearings. Finish off with a lick of paint and it will look as good as new.

As mentioned above, the differential was fitted with a 3.7:1, or occasionally a 4.1:1, ratio.

The three oil seals in the differential are prone to leaking, so it's important to check that the diff is topped up with the correct oil. There are various gear oils on the market but this is one application when EP or extreme pressure oil can be used safely. Also, when fitting new bearings and oil seals to the differential please ensure they are fitted the correct way round

5 The half shafts

The drive shafts on Girling axle cars are pretty robust affairs,

9.7: These Girling half shafts are identifiable by the six-bolt fixings.

although those on the Lockheed type have been known to break. The TR3A's Girling axle is a much stronger component, which really only suffers from weeping oil seals. However, replacement half shafts made from even stronger spec steel are now available from specialist TR suppliers.

The hubs

The early style Lockheed hubs feature ball bearings that were prone to failure due to the limited size of the bearing surface. The later Girling axle cured this problem by having taper roller bearings in a much thicker and stronger hub. The oil seals should always be replaced if ever the hubs are removed on either axle type; the Lockheed ones being especially prone to leak.

Working on and stripping down hubs requires access to presses that the average home garage/DIY mechanic rarely has. For peace of mind remove the hubs yourself by all means, but then take them to a garage that can remove the old ones and press in the new seals and bearings for you. After refitting, don't forget to grease the axle through the grease nipples provided on the axle casing.

Modifications

Changing your Lockheed axle for a Girling one is perhaps the best modification you can do if you have a TR2 or early TR3. It's a much more reliable unit, so unless you desire absolute originality that's the way to go.

The differential can be changed for a limited slip type (LSD). The author has used a plate-type LSD in his various TRs for many years, but other types are available – Salisbury and Quaife LSDs being suitable for a TR.

Finally, there is one other modification that can be done to the Girling axle and that is to replace the steel rear cover on the differential with one from a Triumph 2000. A new oil filler plug will be required, but otherwise it will bolt straight on and it will increase the oil capacity of the differential; useful if you are going continental touring or doing long distance runs as the diff will run cooler.

9.8: A limited-slip differential.

10 The braking system

Overview of the system

When it was first introduced the TR2 was equipped with drum brakes all round. It was fitted with twin 10in x 2¼in shoes at the front, and twin 9in x 1¾in brake shoes at the rear. However, in late 1955, the size of the rear brakes was increased to match those at the front. The 10in rear brake shoe was not without its problems, so later TR3s and all TR3As and TR3Bs reverted to 9in x 1¾in drums.

The braking system starts with the master cylinder, which is located on the bulkhead. The master cylinder is a Lockheed item, which also contains the fluid for the clutch. An internal division prevents brake failure if the clutch develops a leak. A pipe passes down the front of the bulkhead toward a four-way brass union. From this union a flexible hose goes to the OS front wheel, while another pipe passes across the chassis where it meets another connector to operate the hydraulic brakelight switch, and then meets the flexible hose to the NS front

10.1: The original Lockheed brake master cylinder also acts for the clutch.

wheel. The fourth pipe passes back along the chassis to serve the rear brakes. A flexible hose connects this pipe to a three-way connector on the axle in order to allow for movement. The metal brake pipes are held to the chassis by steel clips, and two circular clips fasten the brake pipes to the rear axle.

As a result of Triumph's experience at Le Mans in 1955, 11in diameter disc brakes were introduced in 1956 on the TR3, the first such application on a mass-produced sports car. Although experimental Dunlop disc brakes had been tried on a TR2 at Le Mans, the system chosen for production was made by Girling. A different 'tin can' style master cylinder was introduced (see Fig 10.2) but still with an internal divider for the clutch fluid. Heavy B-series iron callipers were used on the front discs, and these would remain standard equipment even with the introduction of the TR4.

1 Brake fluid

When TR2/3s were rolling off the production line the braking system was filled with a mineral-based brake fluid, but its hygroscopic nature meant that the system could become contaminated with water. Today, many owners will have drained their brake systems and refilled them with silicone-based fluid, which does not attract moisture. This prevents any internal corrosion of the steel brake pipes, but it is important that the two types of fluid are not mixed as they are incompatible. If you're contemplating upgrading your system to use silicone fluid in your car then it's important to flush the mineral oil completely from the system. This is easier said than done, but an air line does make the job easier. Also, mineral oil ought to be changed at regular service intervals, which are usually every three years or 30,000 miles, but with classic cars rarely making such mileage these days it's better to check your system out at the start of every year.

Finally, mineral fluid should never come into contact with the paintwork of your car. If it does, clean it off immediately with warm water as it can be a very effective paint remover! Silicone fluids, you will be glad to hear, don't have such a nasty side-effect.

2 The master cylinder
The fluid reservoirs sitting on top of the bulkhead are among the first things you see on opening the bonnet of a TR2/3. The bulkhead contains mountings for both types of master cylinder, and the two are easily identified by the size and shape of the reservoirs: the early type brake master cylinder essentially being a brass box, while the later type has an upright 'tin can' reservoir (see Fig 10.2).

It's important to

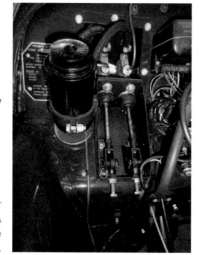

10.2: The Girling master cylinder setup on this TR3A is easily identified by the 'tin can' fluid reservoir.

regularly check that the brake fluid is at the correct level, as this will drop as brake pads wear. Any sudden drop in levels, or if you experience a 'spongy' pedal, must be investigated immediately, as a fractured brake pipe may be the cause. By and large, though, brake master cylinders are reliable units, but seals can fail. A tell-tale sign of a leak can be from fluid running down the brake pedal inside the car. Removal and replacement of the brake master cylinder is straightforward if you follow the workshop manual.

4 Front drum brakes
Despite what people might think there is nothing inherently wrong with having drum brakes all round on a TR. Drum brakes were fitted to many much more powerful cars in period, the Mercedes 300SL being a good example. That said, drum bakes do not have the stopping power of disc brakes, but a drum-braked TR2/3 is still a safe car to drive quickly as long as the driver adapts his/her style of driving.

The front brakes have two leading shoes of 10in x 2¼in, and these are easily adjustable via the small hole in the brake drum. With the wheel off the car the hub can be rotated until the hole in the brake drum lines up with the internal micram adjuster inside the drum. By using a flat-blade screwdriver, the adjuster needs to be turned until the brake drum ceases to revolve. At that point the adjuster can be turned back one notch, and the brake shoe is then set in the correct position. However, you must remember to do the same for the other brake shoe before going on to adjust the brakes on the other side. The reason for this is that the front brakes have TWO wheel cylinders per brake drum, connected by a bridge pipe, whereas the rear brakes only have one wheel cylinder.

10.3: A LHD TR3 showing its master cylinder arrangement. Note the brake pipe passing over the top of the bulkhead instead of going down to the chassis, as on RHD cars.

5 Front disc brakes

Although disc brakes were invented by Lanchester way back in 1902, another 50 years would pass before they were adopted by BRM and Jaguar on their competition cars. Triumph, therefore, was the first large scale manufacturer of production cars to fit its cars with disc brakes, which, according to Triumph's workshop manual, first appeared on the TR3 in late 1956 from chassis TS13101, although the Triumph parts book lists TS13046 for the change.

The TR3/3A and 3B were fitted with disc rotors of 11in diameter. The first

10.5: An early TR3 'A' type one-piece calliper. Note the screw-in cap where the piston goes.

10.4: This TR2 has an alloy spacer fitted to the cast iron brake drum in order for it to accept a non-standard alloy wheel. The hole in the top of the drum is for the brake shoe adjuster.

10.6 (above): This is a type 'B' series calliper as fitted to the TR3, with 11in disc brakes. The red paint is non-standard.

10.7 (right): New callipers are available ... at a price!

such equipped cars were fitted solid Girling 'A' type callipers. These can be identified by a screw in 'plug' where the pistons are fitted (see Fig 10.5). The later Girling 'B' type callipers don't have this plug, as they were cast in two halves (see Fig 10.6). The discs themselves are attached to the front hubs by four bolts. They also have a similar sized dust plate fitted to the inside of the disc.

The calliper houses just two pistons, one on each side of the disc, and, for their time, they had pretty good stopping power. The brake pads on both 'A' and 'B' type callipers are held in place by retaining plates and two set screws.

Approximately 70% of the braking effort is undertaken by the front brakes, and there are several ways in which the front brakes can be upgraded. The easiest upgrade is to cross-drill the discs, as this will aid the removal of water, gas and brake dust, but it will not radically improve braking performance. To do that you either fit thicker, ventilated discs, with an appropriate wider calliper, or, better still, fit larger diameter discs and larger callipers. If you don't want to go down this route then it's also possible to upgrade the standard callipers from two-pot to three- or four-pot pistons. There are a number of conversion kits on the market, available from the various TR specialists, but these will cost you both time and money. Improving the brakes is, however, one of the first things you should consider doing if you want to tune your car for fast road use or competition.

5 Rear drum brakes

With the car jacked up and the rear wheels removed the rear brake drums are exposed. These are cast iron units held in place by two countersunk machine screws. With the handbrake off – and remembering to chock the front wheels – the drums can be eased off to expose the backplate, brake shoes, adjusters and

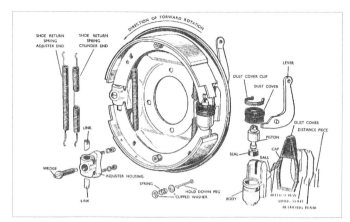

10.8: A diagram showing the key parts of a TR's rear drum brakes.

10.9: A TR3A rear drum brake and hub.

the dual-action piston. In normal service all that's required is the removal of any accumulated brake dust and dirt. Replacing the brake shoes is a simple affair if you follow the workshop manual. A dab of grease on the shoe pivot points will help, but take care not to get any on the brake linings themselves. There isn't much you can do to improve the brakes themselves, but the drums can be replaced with Alfin-type alloy drums, which are available from a number of TR specialists.

6 The handbrake (parking brake)

The sidescreen TRs adhered to a well proven system with a large 'fly-off' handbrake lever protruding from the floorpan, by the right-hand side of the gearbox tunnel. A rubber gaiter seals the

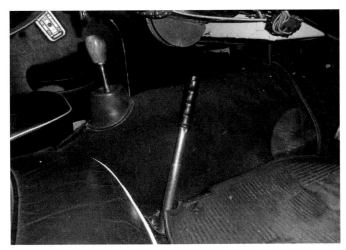

10.10: The fly-off handbrake of a TR3A. No problem for drivers of LHD cars. but it can chafe your left leg on RHD cars.

area of the floorpan where the brake lever comes through, and this gaiter is secured by a metal plate and self tapping screws. The workings of this handbrake all take place under the floor of the car. Its principal fixing is the pivot bolt, which fixes it to the car's chassis. At the other end of the main handbrake cable a compensator bracket and lever fixed to the live axle complete the rest of the linkage to the rear drums. Adjusting the rear brake shoes automatically readjusts the handbrake mechanism, so looking after the brakes should keep the handbrake in good working order.

Remember, though, that handbrake function is an important part of the MOT (roadworthiness) test, so make sure it's maintained in good working order.

7 Brakelight operation

As mentioned earlier, on RHD TR2s the brakelight switch is plumbed into the brake pipe system by a brass coupling down by the front NS brake hose. Being an hydraulic switch, It operates the brake lights when pressure is applied to the brake pedal, forcing fluid into the switch and making an electrical connection. On RHD TR3s, this switch was moved to the front OS of the chassis, and plumbed into a new three-way coupling. Out of sight is often out of mind, so it's worth checking that this switch is in good working order if the brake lights are playing up.

Brake problems

Leaks, noises, vibration, and poor control are all symptoms of a problem that can be traced back to the brakes.

Loss of brake fluid from the main reservoir has been covered already, but leaks can occur at any pipe union, at the rear wheel cylinders, the callipers, and at the flexible hoses. Excessive brake pedal travel is another sign of a possible leak within the system.

10.11: Although covered in dirt and grime, you can just make out the brake switch on this TR3A.

Any sign of such a leak needs to be attended to immediately.

Noisy brakes can be an indication that the brake lining material is seriously worn. What you can hear is the metal part of the brake pad scouring the disc or the rivets of the brake shoe making contact with the iron drum. Immediate replacement of the affected parts is the only answer.

Vibration under braking can also be caused by badly worn brake drums and/or discs. Disc brakes that are showing signs of wear will seriously affect braking performance, and scored discs are a sign of uneven pad wear. The brake pedal will feel uncomfortable under pressure. Remember, too, that brake discs can and will rust if left unused for long periods. On a car that has been left standing over the winter, for example, the brake pads can even be found to have seized onto the disc. A scored disc can be skimmed, but TR discs are not very thick to begin with, and with new discs readily available I feel it's a false economy to skim them. In any event no more than 0.06in should be taken off.

It's also advisable to check the run-out on the disc as it's possible for a disc to warp if subjected to very heavy braking and sudden cooling. Run-out can be done with a dial gauge, and discs should not be more than 0.004in out of true. Similarly, the rear brake drums can wear to an oval shape, and, while these, too, can be machined back to true, fitting a new iron or even an Alfin-type drum would be an easier fix.

If the car pulls to one side under braking it could be due to uneven wear on the front pads, a sticking piston in the brake calliper or even a leak on the opposite side. If the brakes check out okay, then other causes need to be investigated. Try checking the tyre pressures and look for mismatched front tyres, or worn steering or suspension components.

If the brakes aren't releasing correctly, the cause may be a sticking or seized wheel cylinder at the rear, but another culprit might be a deteriorating flexible hose. While it might look okay on the outside, the hose material might be flaking on the inside and acting as a sort of non-return valve. Stainless steel braided hoses are a popular replacement for rubber hoses, and sets are readily available.

Overall, regular servicing and inspection of all the braking system components will ensure that you have trouble-free motoring. A bit of grease goes a long way in keeping the system in good condition, and cars that are laid up for the winter need to be paid greater attention when being put back on the road again in the spring.

Finally, don't forget to check the pipework for corrosion. Older cars often had their brake pipes covered in underseal, which can conceal badly corroded pipes. If rebuilding the car then it's a good idea to replace all the steel pipework with Kunifer pipe. This

10.12: Brake servo.

10.13: Twin system brake setup.

is a copper alloy, and is much stronger than some of the pure copper brake pipe kits that are available.

Modifications

The iron rear drums on all of the sidescreen cars can be replaced with Alfins. These are alloy drums but with iron liners. They were a very popular fitment in the 1950s and '60s, and today there are modern versions available.

TR2s can be modified to take disc brakes, as Triumph did with the TR3, and many cars have already been converted in this way.

Different brake lining material can be employed, both on the discs and on the shoes.

Finally, a restrictor valve that maintains a low pressure in the hydraulic system, and thereby reduces pedal travel prior to braking, could be a worthwhile modification if your car doesn't already have one fitted. They were introduced during TR3 production, but, for some reason, were deleted toward the end of TR3A production.

11 Wheels & tyres

When the TR2 was launched, in 1953, the standard wheel fitted to the car was a steel one of 4J x 15in diameter. The rims were riveted to the centres, which had 12 holes punched into them in three groups of four. A knock-on chrome hub cap, retained by three pegs, was fitted to the wheel, and this should also have a Triumph 'globe' medallion bolted at the centre. This medallion is often missing, however, probably as a result of re-chroming the hub cap, but replacements are readily available on the web.

The wheels were usually painted to match the colour of the bodywork. Experience in competitions soon showed that the riveted wheels were not up to the job, though, and they were soon replaced with welded steel rims.

As the steel wheels were only painted, rust can be a problem if left to go unchecked. Shot blasting and powder coating can rectify that, though. What is harder to rectify is a buckled wheel rim caused by kerbing. A buckled rim can cause steering vibration, and both sides of the wheel should be checked for damage.

11.1: A standard TR wheel complete with chrome hubcap with the Triumph 'world' logo in the centre.

11.2: Allowing rust to build up on a riveted wheel is not a good idea.

11.3: Having the wheels shot blasted and then powder coated can transform them.

As mentioned above, early TR steel wheels can be had with either a riveted rim or welded construction. The photo in Fig 11.2 shows a riveted rim that was on the author's own TR. On the outside it looked a perfectly good wheel, but, as the picture shows, it was very rusty on the inside. This just goes to show that it's worth taking the wheels off your car every so often to give them a good clean and brush up, if only to protect them from rust.

Wire wheels
Steel wheels featured on the majority of sidescreen cars sold throughout the production run, with only about 15% being ordered with the optional 48-spoke wire wheels. However, 48 spoke wires tend to flex under hard cornering, so, with experience gained from the works rally team, in 1958 a stronger 60-spoke wire wheel was introduced for the TR3A.

These stronger wheels can easily be retrofitted to those TR3 cars fitted with the Girling axle. However, TR2s and early TR3s fitted with a Lockheed axle pose more of a problem, as they used a different type of splined hub carrier. These Lockheed type hub carriers are quite rare these days, so, given the inherent weakness of the 'Mayflower' axle that was used in the early TR2/3, my advice would be to change the whole assembly for the stronger Girling 'Vanguard' type axle that was introduced in 1956 at chassis number TS13046.

11.4: These 48-spoke wires might be easier to clean, but they lack the strength of later wheels.

Wire wheels were usually painted silver or aluminium in colour by the factory, but the author has seen several cars sporting black or white wire wheels. These were probably repainted later by their owners and not by the factory, but with Triumph anything was possible.

Since wire wheels require special splined hub adaptors to be fitted to the hubs, it's worth noting that fitting these adaptors marginally increases the width of the track. Furthermore, the standard length wheel studs need to be cut down if you are converting a steel wheeled car to run on wires, and special chamfered nuts are required to fit the new hub adaptors. However, it is possible to fit a ¼in spacer over the studs, which will avoid the need to cut the studs down, but you will still need the chamfered nuts. These spacers will also place a bit more load on the wheel bearings and make the track wider still.

Wires can undoubtedly transform the look of your car, but they do require much more maintenance than steel wheels. Cleaning a wire wheel properly is a very time-consuming task, and, even with the aid of a power washer it can be hard to remove all traces of brake dust that collects by the spokes. Wire wheels are also more prone to accident damage from kerbing. A buckled wire wheel will make the steering seem very heavy indeed, while 'clunks' in the driveline under acceleration and braking can also be an indication of worn splines.

The spokes can come loose, and the locating splines can wear badly if not properly lubricated. Chrome wires are also more susceptible to breakage, as the chroming process makes the steel more brittle.

As a result it's advisable not to used chromed wires on competition cars

The author knows this only too well, as, after competing in a hillclimb, he once found 15 loose or broken spokes in one of the

11.5: The splined hub adaptor for fitting wire wheels. It's important to keep these well greased with Copaslip™ or some other suitable grease. Note also the use of chamfered nuts to hold the adaptor to the hub.

11.6: A 60-spoke painted wire wheel.

69

11.7: A 72-spoke wire flexes a lot less than a 60-spoke wheel, and so is much safer for competition work.

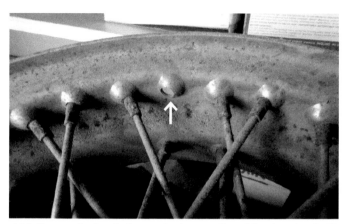

11.8: Even a single missing spoke (arrowed) on this wire wheel will affect its balance and strength.

chrome wire wheels on his TR4. This was surprising as there was no apparent change in the car's handling. Only a tinkling sound led him to inspect the wheels. Regular inspection of your wires is to be recommended. In my case, a change to the much stronger 72-spoke painted wires soon followed!

Original wire wheels also required the use of an inner tube, but modern wires can now run tubeless tyres as they are fitted with a nylon band that covers the spoke fittings in the well of the wheel.

Balancing a wire wheel correctly is very important and not every tyre fitter has the correct cone adaptor to allow them to spin the wheels up to speed. Modern balancing machines, though, can now measure run out accurately, and balance both the inside and outside of the wheel.

The splined hub and the wheel itself can wear badly if they're not kept well greased. It's also important to tighten the splined hub nuts to the correct torque. If they work loose, then both the wheel and the splined hub may become detached from the car, with disastrous consequences.

Finally, the splined adaptors are handed, so make sure you have them fitted onto the correct hub. The author once found to his cost and great embarrassment – but to the great amusement of his friends – that, in a rush to complete the car in time for a rally, he had fitted the hubs on his newly rebuilt TR4 on the wrong side! After a fast journey of some 130 miles he found the large centre lock wheel spinners had been slowly coming undone! Clearly this shouldn't have happened, since

11.9: The three-eared knock-on/off spinners are clearly marked as to which side they must go.

Of course, fitting such wheels today can offend the purist, but they were of their time and the cars were our daily drivers back then. In fact genuine Wolfrace and Cosmic wheels are now highly sought-after and can command a decent price on eBay.

11.10: Chris Sergison's TR2 fitted with slotted Wolfrace wheels. We all thought they looked pretty cool back then.

the standard chrome two-eared spinners are clearly marked as to which side they should be on and which way they should be done up.

Aftermarket wheels

It's well known that wheels can transform the look of your car. Alloy wheels became quite a popular fitment in the 1970s, and quite a few TRs started to wear Cosmic or Wolfrace alloys as a replacement for old and troublesome wires, as this picture (Fig 11.10) of a TR2 taken in 1977 shows.

A more popular alloy wheel today is the Minilte replica. With its eight large spokes it is much easier to keep clean, and its rugged looks complement rather than detract from the TRs appearance. However, being alloy they are more susceptible to kerbing and alloy corrosion, which can cause problems in sealing the tyre bead to the rim.

However, whatever type of wheel you choose it's important not to go overboard on them, and to pay attention to wheel offsets. A wider rim width of up to 5in can easily be accommodated by a TR2/3/3A, but having too large a wheel can place a severe strain on suspension components and that can lead to front suspension failure.

Of course, if it's originality you're after, and you can't be bothered with the hassle of cleaning wire wheels, then the period aftermarket wheel trims, shown in Fig 11.13, might be the

11.11: A genuine magnesium alloy Minilite wheel. They are even lighter than the alloy replicas, but should be crack tested before being fitted.

11.13: 'Ace' wheel discs were a popular period accessory.

answer. Made of bright anodised pressed alloy they certainly look the part but are hard to find these days.

11.12: This TR3A has been fitted with 5in TR6 rims, painted white to contrast with the body colour.

Tyres

Goodyear, Dunlop and Michelin all supplied tyres for the TR2-3, with the standard size being a 5.50 x 15 crossply tyre. Later, radial tyres of 165 x 15 section would become the norm for UK markets, but it took some time before the USA adopted the radial tyre.

Tyre technology advanced greatly during the production life of the TR, and Michelin X tyres were often the tyre of choice for competition motoring as they were noted for their longer life due to a harder rubber compound.

The best advice is to always buy the best tyre you can afford, as it's the only thing that keeps you in contact with the road.

Low profile tyres might look good on a modern Euro box, but on a TR they place an enormous amount of strain on suspension systems that were not designed for it. The tyres on any classic car should fill the wheelarch otherwise the car can end up looking under-tyred. The grip from low profile tyres might be fantastic, but they can also let go without warning, too! Early TRs were designed in an age of crossply tyres, which allowed for sliding around corners and were much more forgiving. Radial tyres fitted to a TR2/3 can give much greater cornering performance, but modern tyre compounds can exceed even those design limits. Understeer can quickly give way to oversteer, with unforeseen consequences.

It's also a good idea to take the wheels off the car if it is to be laid up for the winter, and lay the tyres flat in order to avoid flat-spotting them. Finally, rather than filling the tyres with air, try to find a tyre dealer who will fill them with inert nitrogen. Air contains water vapour, whereas nitrogen is a pure gas and pressures can be maintained more easily.

Of course, taking off the wheels will mean jacking up the car. For some reason Triumph in its wisdom decided it would be a good idea to be able to jack up the car from INSIDE the car! The factory supplied pillar jack that does this is a rare find these days,

11.14: The internal jacking point. There is one on each side of the chassis

and has usually been replaced with either a small bottle or scissor jack kept inside the dish of the spare wheel. However, if you do happen to have an original jack it works by removing one of the two large rubber bungs in the floorpan and locating it into the chassis fitting.

12 Electrical system & instruments

General observations

All TRs use Lucas 12-volt electrical systems, and there is a great deal of commonality of parts used between the cars. The TR2-3B used a positive earth return from the battery, but it's possible to convert them to the more common negative earth system. Power was generated originally by a Lucas C39 PV-2 dynamo driven from the crankshaft pulley. Later this was changed to a Lucas C40 unit. The two dynamos can be distinguished by the later type having push-on connectors rather than screw-on terminals. An alternator was never offered as an option, not even on the later TR3A, but plenty of owners have converted to one these days, the author included. An electrical regulator was mounted on the bulkhead, as was the fusebox, which has the main circuits protected by twin fuses. The fusebox also has provision for two spare fuses to be carried internally. Electrical gremlins do rear their heads from time to time, and because wiring looms will have been altered so as to add extra electrical items, the loom can deteriorate over time. However, it's usually one of the last things owners tend to replace because it usually means stripping out the car. Early looms were fabric-covered but later items were wrapped in plastic. There are also some differences in the type of connectors used, so it's worth checking which sort you have before you buy a new loom. This is easily done by looking at the regulator, which is also fitted on the bulkhead along with the flasher unit and starter solenoid. On the early cars the regulator has screw terminal fittings but later cars have spade terminals. The regulator, which is a Lucas RB106/1 unit, can be mounted vertically or horizontally,

12.1: An original style wet cell battery. The starter solenoid, fusebox, and voltage regulator can also be seen.

depending on the age of the car.

Three types of flasher unit were employed during the TR2/3's production run, these being Lucas FL2, FL3 and last of all the FL5 with spade connectors. The solenoid has a push button on one end, which aids starting when you're messing around under the bonnet. A lot of solenoids these days don't have this feature, so it's worth tracking one down if you can.

Instrumentation came courtesy of Jaeger, and featured black dials with white numerals set in chrome bezels. Convex glass was used on all dials. Toggle switches operated the lights, panel illumination and wipers. These are located, together with the choke control and starter button, on the centre panel. The overdrive switch, when fitted, could either be a toggle or a flick switch mounted on the dashboard.

Common problems

1 The battery

The TR's battery is located in a well built into the bulkhead. While this allows for very easy everyday access and a much shorter lead to the starter motor, the battery can and does get hot, especially in summer when ambient temperatures are much higher. On a traditional lead acid battery this can lead to the distilled water evaporating, so a regular check should be made to see if topping up is required. Distilled water used to be readily available from the garage forecourt, but most garages now seem to be more interested in selling coffee rather than aids to motoring. You can obtain your own supply of distilled water simply by defrosting the ice build up in your freezer! Alternatively, you should be able to buy it over the counter at a motoring stores. Do not use tap water!

Because modern batteries now tend to be sealed for life you can't really maintain them, but a periodic check with a multimeter should see an output of more than 12 volts. One thing you can do on whatever type of battery you have is to make sure the battery posts are kept clean (the same can be said for the battery lead caps or clamps). The author recommends a good smear of petroleum jelly, and, if possible, fitting some colour-coded rubber terminal covers to keep dirt away and make it easy to identify which terminal is which. It would be all too easy for someone to try to jump start your car not realising it had a positive earth!

Something else that is often overlooked is the condition of the earth strap. On the TR2/3 the earth strap runs down to the chassis from the front plate of the engine. The bolts securing it to the engine and the chassis should be kept clean. Do check that

there isn't any paint where the strap makes contact. Experience has shown that after a rebuild and respray, a poor earth connection here can cause starting difficulties.

12.2: Often overlooked, the earth strap is a vital bit of the TR's electrics.

Finally, do make sure that the battery is kept secure at all times. The angle bracket provided does a good job on a standard size battery, but modern smaller batteries may be more difficult to secure. Fitting a plastic battery tray underneath the battery is always a good idea, as is to clearly mark the battery terminals: Red for positive and Black or Yellow for negative.

2 Jump leads and trickle charging

Cars that don't get a lot of use tend to have weak batteries, and may require a jump start or the use of a portable starter pack to get them going. Good quality jump leads are hard to find, but are easily identified by their relatively heavy weight. The thin wire leads that often come with some of the emergency packs sold at retail outlets are not really robust enough.

When jump starting from another car make sure that the leads are fitted correctly and that the cable clamps don't touch any part of either car's engine or bodywork. Also remember that sidescreen TRs should be positively earthed.

With the rescue car's engine running it should now be possible to start your own car. The rescue car should be run up to about 1500rpm in order to offer a good output

12.3: Use heavy-duty jump leads and keep a trickle charger to hand if you don't use the car regularly.

from its own charging system. Once it has started, disconnect the battery leads from your own car first, again making sure the clamps don't touch the engine, bodywork or each other. It's then safe to remove the clamps from the other car.

Charging a battery with a mains powered battery charger should really be done with the battery taken off the car. Batteries can give off fumes from the electrolyte – sulphuric acid – so charging should be carried out in a well ventilated place. Do NOT breathe in any fumes, and, if you're unfortunate enough to spill battery acid on yourself wash it off immediately as it's very corrosive.

Trickle charging is now a very popular method of keeping a car battery in good condition. There are a variety of devices on the market, but those giving a clear indication of the charging level are among the most useful.

When trickle charging make sure the connections are made correctly, and only turn on the power after the battery has been connected. Trickle chargers can be left on for long periods of time but batteries work best when they can discharge and recycle, so once it's topped up why not take the car out for a run?

3 Battery acid spillage

If a plastic battery box or spill tray has been fitted, then any spillage from the battery should be safely contained. If the battery is just sitting in the well in the bulkhead, then not only can the paintwork be damaged but the acid can attack the steelwork under it.

4 Battery security

I've mentioned above the need to keep the battery secured. Whilst the clamp provided will prevent it from moving about in normal day-to-day driving, in the event of an accident, and should the car overturn, that clamp might not be sufficient. The addition of some sturdy tie wraps looped over the top of the battery would improve things. Please make sure that the terminal clamps are bolted on tight. A clamp that comes adrift in an accident could short out, and, if there's a fuel leak from the engine ... well, best not to dwell on that.

5 The charging system
The dynamo's job is to provide electricity to run the car's electrical systems and to keep the battery charged. The standard C39 PV-2 and C40 dynamos fitted to the TR2/TR3 can do that job. However, if you're adding extras, such as an electric fan, spot lights, a modern radio, phone charger or a satellite navigation system to the car, then the standard dynamo as fitted by Triumph is not really up to the job. I would therefore recommend fitting an alternator if you have all these extra gadgets fitted to your car.

Fortunately, TRs are fitted with a +/- 30 amp ammeter, so you can see if the car is being charged correctly. The needle should always show a positive charge, apart from on starting when it will, of course, show a discharge as the starter motor cranks over the engine.

12.4: This dynamo has a broken front mounting lug. It's a common fault and so it's time to replace it.

12.5: A dynamo is now a rare sight on any TR, but for those who like originality it's possible to fit an alternator like this that looks just like a dynamo.

The greatest load on a charging system is at night when everything is operating. The headlights will be on, the wipers will be on if it's raining, the heater blower, if fitted, will be doing its best to try and de-mist the windscreen, and the aforementioned spot lights and satnav systems will all be requiring power, and it is the dynamo's job to provide it.

Dynamos are pretty reliable units but, like all things mechanical, they can fail. The dynamo is driven by the fanbelt, and care must be taken not to run it too slack, or, even worse, too tight! Over tensioning the fanbelt can put strain on the dynamo bearings, and this is usually accompanied by a loud screeching noise.

The good thing about a dynamo, though, is that it is very easy to rebuild it. In today's world where real garage mechanics have been replaced by computer diagnostics and fitters who replace whole parts rather than fixing them, it's good to know that a dynamo can be rebuilt on a home work bench. Usually all that ever needs replacing are the carbon brushes, which are readily available and cheap. However, if it does need a strip down then it's a simple and satisfying job to clean the carbon build up off the commutator and replace the bearings.

If you do decide to replace your dynamo then there a number of options available to you. You can upgrade to a much higher amp rated alternator that looks just like an original dynamo. This will require a few minor wiring modifications to the regulator and plug connectors, or you can consider fitting a smaller lightweight alternator instead, which are available from the many TR specialists (See Fig 12.6).

6 General electrical faults
The wiring system is probably the most neglected part on a

12.6: One of the really small lightweight alternators. It might be small but it still packs a punch!

12.7: The fusebox contains one 50 amp and one 30 amp fuse plus two spare fuses. It should have a plastic cover to protect them. Note the rubber button on the end of the starter solenoid, and the screw terminals on the voltage regulator.

classic car. All of the Lucas spade, screw or bullet connectors are potential weak links in the electrical system, and they can all suffer from corrosion. Those connections that are exposed to road dirt and bad weather are especially susceptible and should be checked first. The fuse holders are protected from the elements, but the connectors are not, and over time many of the clear rubber Lucar spade connector covers split or go missing. A multimeter will help to identify any shortcomings in the circuits, but if the circuit is found to be sound then it's probably the component itself that is at fault.

7 The starter motor

The original equipment starter motor is quite a heavy beast, and if you have to replace it this often requires the removal of the exhaust downpipes to facilitate its removal.

Starter motors can jam, and the old trick of giving it a belt with a copper hammer often released it, but it's not advisable.

The motor draws a lot of current when starting, so it needs the battery to be in good

12.8: An original type of starter motor as fitted to the TR2, 3 and earlier TR3As.

12.9: A much lighter and smaller reduction gear starter motor.

condition if it's to spin the four-cylinder engine. If the engine has been modified with a higher compression ratio, though, this will place even more strain on the motor. My advice is to replace the motor with a much smaller, lighter and more powerful quick start motor (see Fig 12.9). These double reduction-geared units spin the engine much more quickly and draw less current. They are, to my mind, a 'must have,' and both of the author's four- and six-cylinder cars have been so equipped.

8 Instruments & controls

The TR2/3 featured a full-width trimmed dashboard, with the main instruments placed in front of the driver, and the four auxiliary dials and switches placed in a panel in the centre of the dash. TR2/3 centre panels were always trimmed in the same colour material as the dashboard. Only on the TR3A was it changed to a painted crackle black finish.

12.12: Replacing the rev counter. Note the rubber sealing gasket and the spade-type fitting used to retain it behind the dashboard.

12.10 and 12.11: The TR3A dashboard is easily identified by its black crackle centre panel compared to the TR2 dash (top).

Apart from the ammeter, which was supplied by Lucas, Jaeger supplied the rest of the instruments. The dials have white numerals on black faces, and all instruments have domed glasses with chrome bezels.

Replacing gauges on a TR2/3A can be a fiddly process, and generally involves working upside down in the footwell, when trying to undo the knurled nuts and spade screws that retain the instruments. However, the panel holding the minor instruments can be removed by undoing the four nuts holding it in place. With the centre panel removed, you can also access the back of the speedo and rev counter more easily. The fabric-covered dash is actually fixed to the scuttle by half a dozen bolts, and can be removed for retrimming if required.

TR speedos are marked with a calibration number under the mileage indicator. This should read 1180 for a car with the standard 3.7:1 rear axle ratio, which is the number of speedo cable revolutions per mile. As many cars now run on radial tyres rather than the original crossplies, the rolling radius of the tyre will be slightly different, so the speedo will either read under or over. Different final drive ratios will also affect the speedo reading. It's worth bearing this in mind as speed cameras don't make any allowance for this!

Rev counters are mechanical units driven from the distributor, but can be replaced with electronic items if so desired, usually in conjunction with fitting a solid state distributor, which eliminates the need for a drive cable.

If the drive cables are retained for the speedo and rev counter, it pays to attend to how they are routed in order to avoid kinking and/or chafing as they pass through the bulkhead. The speedo cable is particularly susceptible to damage as it can hang down under the car's chassis.

The angle drive can also be a weak point on the speedo drive. As cables wear the needles tend to fluctuate or bounce, so accurate reading can be a problem.

The odometer (trip meter) built into the speedometer is also prone to wear. This is indicated by the numerals not lining up exactly, caused by the drive teeth becoming worn as drivers reset the trip to zero. The numerals on the total mileage recorder should remain in line. If they don't line up then the mileage might well have been altered to give a lower reading. On a car that is over 50 years old this is not really a problem, as it has probably gone around the clock anyway and it is unlikely that the mileage reading will be an important factor in your decision to buy it. However, on a car that is being advertised with a 'genuine low mileage' it's always worth checking.

The oil pressure gauge should read quite high on starting as oil pressure builds up. 80-100psi is quite normal. During normal running the oil pressure should never be less than 40psi at 2000rpm hot. Any reading lower than that is a likely indication that the main bearings are worn.

The fuel gauge is operated from a sender in the fuel tank. This sender is a reliable unit, but if it does need to be replaced then

12.13: The speedometer is driven by a cable that fits into the gearbox casing, as shown by the arrow.

the tank has to be removed to do so. This is a straightforward operation but, as usual, care must be taken to drain fuel from the tank, and it's vitally important to disconnect the battery first. After disconnecting the electrical connections to the sender unit, and the pipe unions that feed into the tank, the tank can be removed by undoing the straps that secure it to the body. After replacing the sender unit and using a new gasket seal, refitting the tank is a reversal of the above procedure.

The water temperature gauge has an electrical connection to its sender, which is mounted in the thermostat housing. The

Lucar connection is easily dislodged, resulting in no reading on the gauge. Other than that or a bulb failure the water temperature gauge is a reliable unit.

The ammeter can give a good indication of the state of the electrical system. A reading of +15-20 amps should be seen on start-up as the charging system feeds back into the battery, and it should maintain a small positive reading (~+2 amps) when driving. If it starts to show a negative reading when driving then trouble is brewing somewhere in the charging system. It may just be a slipping fanbelt caused by a loose dynamo bracket, but having ruled that out then a more serious problem is likely. The tell-tale ignition warning light might also be on – which, of course, it shouldn't be.

Sod's law says that such a charging issue will only ever happen to you at night and when you're miles from anywhere. However, from personal experience, it's possible to drive quite a long way on a fully charged battery, so, if forced to do so, then turn off any unnecessary electrical items to reduce the amount of electricity you use.

Other electrical components that can create problems are the wiper motor and the overdrive switches.

The wipers

The original TR2 wiper motor is a Lucas CRT 15 unit mounted on the left-hand side of the bulkhead as viewed from the front. As you can see it is pretty crowded on this side of the bulkhead, so this was changed to a Lucas DR2 unit from chassis TS15267, and mounted on the right-hand side of the bulkhead.

The screen wipers on the TR2/3 are pretty feeble at the best of times. The single-speed wiper is either off or on, and it doesn't really do a great deal when it is on! While a self-parking two-speed DR3 type wiper was later offered as an optional extra,

12.14 (a and b): Showing the correct resting position for the wipers and the original TR2 Lucas CRT15 wiper motor. Compare the latter's position on the bulkhead to that in the later car in Fig 12.15.

together with a manual screen washer, the fact is that the wipers are not really powerful enough to clear the amount of rain we can get here in the UK. There really isn't very much an owner can do to rectify this state of affairs other than to keep the blades in tip

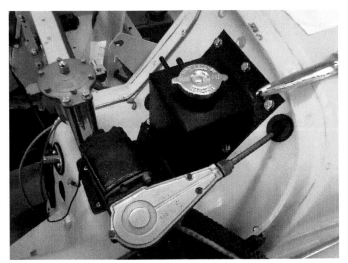

12.15: A single-speed wiper motor now mounted on the other side of the bulkhead. The bulkhead-mounted header tank and fuel filter/pressure regulator are non-standard but good ideas.

top condition and to make sure the springs on the wiper arms keep the blades in contact with the screen. The use of Rain-X on the screen is also recommended.

While replacing a wiper arm is easy, if the wipers do pack up, and the motor and drive rack are not at fault, then the problem will lie in the drive spindles. Replacing these is by access from under the dash.

The spindles are clamped onto the tubes through which the drive rack passes. With the wiper gear removed, make a note of which way the spindles are fixed, as it's all too easy to re-install them upside down!

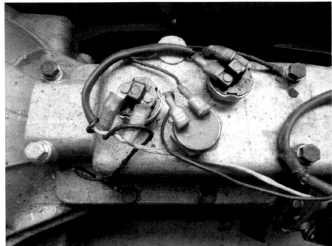

12.16 (above): The isolator switches. Two are for the overdrive and one is for a reversing light, which shows this car is fitted with the later type TR4 gearbox top cover.

12.17 (right): The solenold that operates the overdrive. Note the split in the rubber cover, which, therefore, needs replacing.

12.18: The overdrive switch on a TR3A.

12.19: A TR2 fitted with a period car radio and speaker.

Meanwhile, the overdrive, which operates on second, third and fourth gears, can be plagued by poor connections to the isolator switches mounted on top of the gearbox. To fix those means removing a good portion of the car's interior, so it's a good idea to make sure the switches are shimmed correctly to operate in their respective gears, and, if possible, to wire the connectors in place so that they cannot become loose.

It's also a good idea to make sure the bullet connection to the overdrive solenoid is secure, and that there's enough slack in the overdrive cables feeding out from the gearbox cover up to the dash-mounted overdrive switch, as they have been known to come adrift at the bullet connectors.

Another electrical part that can create a problem is the ignition switch. The barrels can wear over time, and original spec switches with FS series keys are no longer available. The replacement switches that are available are rather poor quality, and don't have a radio position built in to them.

In-car radios were still something of a novelty in the 1950s, and it wasn't until 1954 that Triumph offered a Radiomobile radio as an optional extra. These were first fitted in place of the glovebox lid, the lid being replaced with a suitable radio slot. However, people liked having a lockable glovebox, so later a bracket fitted under the glovebox was utilised, or, as shown in Fig 12.19, positioned over the gearbox tunnel, with an additional speaker mounted above it. Triumph also made provision for a speaker in the footwell.

Finally, one part that always seemed to cause the author trouble was the horn. The Bakelite housing can crack and the wiring is difficult to replace, so quite a few TR owners resorted to fitting air horns instead of rectifying the problem. Cars converted to rack and pinion steering will also need the wiring sorted out if the original horn push is to be retained.

13 Weather equipment & interior trim

13.1: The interior of the author's long-door TR2. The radio console is non-standard.

13.2: A sidescreen as fitted to a TR2. Note the one-piece plastic window. Compare this to the much later TR3A sidescreen in figure 13.3.

13.3: A TR3A sidescreen. Note the sliding window and the door handle, which obviated the need to lift the bottom part of the screen in order to open the door.

Compared to what rival car maker MG had to offer in 1954, the TR2 introduced a new level of comfort in UK sports car design. Triumph was well ahead of its main competitor who, twelve months later, was still building the 1500cc MGTF, which still featured what was basically prewar styling.

Unlike the MG, the TR2 could be ordered with a hardtop, which, when fitted correctly, turned the open sports car into a snug little coupé, and made the car eligible to compete in the then hotly contested GT classes. Early factory hardtops were made of polyester resin, not fibreglass as some say. Later, a factory steel hardtop became available, but a number of fibreglass hardtops also appeared from aftermarket companies like Ashley and Lenham.

While the sidescreens were a notable feature of the TR, a hardtop equipped TR was thought to be a more sophisticated model that would appeal to a more discerning buyer who wanted the feel of a traditional sports car but without the hassle of putting a hood up and down.

On the roadster version, the TR2/3 retained a separate hood that could be stored in the boot when not in use. The hood frame then folded down into the well behind the seats.

Common problems

The TR2/3 owner is fortunate in that nearly all of the trim fitted to the cars is still available, albeit in mostly reproduction rather than original form. Generally, there's a good supply of trim parts to be found, and there are several items that can offer an improvement over the original offering from Triumph.

Worn out carpets are easy to replace on the TR, but finding original spec material for the TR2 is quite hard. New door cards can also be fitted by a DIY owner, if care is taken when doing so. Replacing a worn out or torn hood and tonneau cover is a more complicated affair, which can be done at home but is best carried out by a professional trimmer. It's important to keep the hood in good condition as leaks will affect the interior trim. Sodden carpets and under felts will hasten the onset of rust in the floors and sills, and they will be much more expensive to replace! The Vybak plastic rear windows can become opaque, and are 'welded' into the hood material. There are some products available that claim to restore the clarity of Vybak windows, but if

they are that bad then the sensible option is to replace the hood completely.

When replacing trim owners have the option to upgrade it to whatever they fancy. Leather seats, Wilton carpets and mohair hoods are all available; it just depends on your taste and the size of your wallet.

The hardtop

The TR2/3's hardtop was a one-piece affair with either a Perspex or glass window. Steel hardtops are fixed to the rear deck by five bolts, and to the windscreen header rail by two more fixings. Anodised alloy rain channels are fitted around the door openings, and the interior should have a cotton cloth headlining.

13.4: One of the works rally cars fitted with its hardtop. Note the extra alloy clips fitted top and bottom of the rear window to prevent it popping out.

The hood and tonneau cover

As roadsters, all sidescreen TRs came with a completely detachable hood that could be stowed behind the seats or in the boot.

Hoods were available in a variety of colours, even geranium pink, though it was usual to match the hood to the paintwork, and black, white or beige vinyl seemed to be the most popular.

13.5: The white vinyl hood and sidescreens on this TR3A contrast nicely with the dark blue bodywork.

Today many a TR can be seen sporting a posh mohair hood in black, blue, red, tan or green, with a matching tonneau cover.

Early cars had only one rear clear plastic window, but later hoods had three plastic windows fitted to aid rear visibility when reversing. There was also an optional full length tonneau cover and a smaller hood cover available. The hoods on the first TR2s were affixed by small Tenax fasteners, which are now very difficult to come by. The factory soon changed these to the larger 'lift the dot' fasteners, and these are readily available today.

All hoods benefit from regular cleaning with warm soapy water and/or vinyl cleaner. The zip on the tonneau cover is often neglected, and the fasteners can become detached from the vinyl. If the zip does break it's worth checking out the price of a replacement, as it's a simple job for a trimmer to replace it. If you can get hold of a brass zip rather than a plastic one then so much the better. Failing that, Velcro could be used, but

that would require another flap of material to be sewn onto the tonneau cover.

Finally, it's worth noting that quite a lot of cars are now being fitted with Mazda MX5 seats (see Fig 13.11). In that case the tonneau covers need to be altered to accommodate the headrests.

13.6: The erected hood frame. Note that the webbing straps utilise longer pegs on the rear deck in order to fit them over the 'lift the dot' fasteners.

Carpets

There were two different types of carpet offered by Triumph. Initially, carpets had a wool pile, but these were replaced with nylon loop pile carpets.

The loop pile material used in the TR3A is hard to come by today, so most owners now fit 'Wilton' wool style carpet sets. However, taking care of the carpets is a good idea no matter what the material, and regular brushing and vacuuming is all that is required on a day-to-day basis.

Wet carpets can introduce rust to the floorpans, so it's advisable to remove them in order to dry them out thoroughly. This is not as straightforward as it seems, though, because to remove the carpets from under the seats requires that the seats and seat runners themselves be removed first. The floor, gearbox tunnel and almost all of the other carpets are held in place by press studs, so their removal is easy. The carpets on the sides of the footwells, though, are either held in place by screws or glued into position, as are those behind the seats. These carpets should be removed with care as the carpet can tear, but they can be fixed back into to position with spray glue or similar. Leaving them in place if wet is definitely NOT a good idea!

The boot floor of the TR2/3 was also fitted with carpet, and a card/millboard back panel hides the fuel tank from view. A lot of cars now have a fully carpeted boot but, while the boot seal offers a good fit, leaks are not uncommon and so the same applies to any carpet you have in there; just keep it clean and dry. Finally, if the floor carpets have got wet then it's more than likely that so will the underfelts. Again, dry them well before refitting, and, if desired, some extra floor sound deadening material can be introduced at the same time.

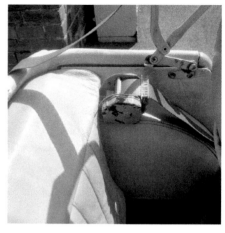

13.7: This is a very neat installation of Citroën inertia reel seatbelts on a TR3A.

Seatbelts

TRs didn't have seatbelts fitted when new. In fact, it wasn't until 1965 that UK manufacturers were compelled to fit them, and then it was only to the front seats of cars. Rear seat passengers had to wait until 1991 before UK law required them to belt up. While it's not against the law to drive a TR2/3 that's never been fitted with seatbelts it is advisable to fit them.

If seatbelts are to be fitted then the anchor points should be on the inside or on top of the rear wheelarches, the bottom of the B-posts, and each side of the transmission tunnel. Seatbelts can be lap and diagonal, and either tensioned by the occupant or inertia reels, as shown in Fig 13.7.

In any open-topped car seatbelts can get wet and they should be allowed to dry out thoroughly. If badly stained they can be cleaned with warm soapy water, but if they become frayed at all then they must be replaced.

The seats

Compared to those in other contemporary makes of sports car, TR seats, with their sprung seat cushions and rounded bucket-style backs, were considered to be very comfortable. They were also adjustable for fore and aft movement, so the seat runners will benefit from some lubrication from time to time. However, care should be taken not to lubricate the carpets!

As the seats bolt to the runners it's a good idea to reinforce the seat pans where the bolts go through with some penny washers. These can be brazed on rather than welded, and will help to stop cracks appearing in the seat pans, as getting in out of the car places a great deal of strain on these mounting points.

TR2s had fixed seat backs, but owners who ordered their TR3/3A or 3B with the optional rear seat found that the back of the passenger seat could now tip forward to facilitate access.

Even so, it must have been a tight squeeze for children, let alone an adult to get in the back of a TR, especially if the hood was up or a hardtop was in place.

Apart from the usual tears and splits that come with frequent use, TR seats generally stand up well over time. They do have a removable seat cushion made up of steel springs and stuffed with horse hair and wadding. Over time the springs can sag and break, and the seat pan can be devoured by rust. Original style seat cushions are available, though a good trimmer can easily replace this style of seat cushion with a much more comfortable one made up of multiple layers of different density foam.

The original pattern Vynide covering material can be replaced with leather seat facings, which were always a factory option. Alternatively, you could replace the TR seats completely. As mentioned previously, Mazda MX5 seats are a very popular option as they're quite narrow, recline, and even offer the options of a built in seat heater and loudspeakers! A different subframe is required if you go down this route, and, of course, the tonneau cover will need work if it's to fit over the high back MX5 seat (see Fig 13.11).

13.8: Compare these TR2/3 seats with those from the later TR3A below. The vertical pleating and a thin edge to the seatback are the obvious differences.

13.9: The TR3A featured restyled seats with greater padding, but were they any more comfortable?

13.10: A TR3 rear seat. Post TS 60001 TR3As had a different style of seat due to changes in the bodywork.

13.11: MX5 seats have been fitted to this TR3A. Without a doubt they are far more comfortable than the standard issue.

Seals, trim panels and door cards

If everything is kept in fine fettle the cabin of the TR2/3 can be a joy to be in. One shouldn't expect the same level of comfort that we get from modern cars, so draughts are to be expected. The door seals and the furflex trim around them should be replaced as necessary. Badly fitting seals around the windscreen are liable to leak, and if you are not intending to remove the windscreen then a bead of clear silicone sealant on the lower screen rubber can help to secure it in place.

Most of the trim on a TR2/3 is easily replaced, so scuffs and tears can be fixed. Both types used similar door cards, with a pocket built in, but door release pulls were visible on the inside of TR2/3 doors, whereas the TR3A/B had them fitted behind the door casing, accessible via the door pocket. This is due to the different types of sidescreens and the absence of external door locks on the TR2/3s.

13.12: The door cards are held in place with screws, and are very easy to maintain. The padded roll on the top of the door is less so.

The hardboard backing of the door cards can warp over time, and pull away from the doors. Replacement is quite straightforward, but do take care when removing and refitting them.

If desired, TR2/3 owners may wish to 'upgrade' their dash by having the central instrument cluster finished in walnut veneer.

Some very early TR2s sported what is known as 'wicker' trim. This is almost certainly impossible to find these days, but would you actually want it on your car? To say it's an acquired taste is an understatement! In fact, the author has only ever seen one example of the type in 50 years of TR motoring.

The windscreen and aeroscreens

Standard TR2/3 windscreens were made by Triplex and featured laminated safety glass. Today, replacement screens are readily available, and can come with a variety of tints, usually green, blue or grey, on the top 3-4in of the screen. The complete windscreen assembly can, of course, be easily removed from the car by undoing the Dzus fasteners on the screen pillars (see Fig 13.14) and sliding it forward off the retaining brackets. It's really a two man job to do this, though, in order to avoid damaging the paintwork.

Fitting a new glass to the windscreen frame is quite a difficult job, and my advice would be to let an expert do it. The tolerances are very small and the set screws, which may have been in place for over 60 years, can be very hard to undo. The majority of a screen's metalwork is made of chrome-plated brass, but alloy stanchions were also fitted to the TR3A, so don't try re-chroming these!

However, if you do decide to take off the screen, you can fit aeroscreens, and experience real wind in your hair motoring – not to mention the flies in your teeth! TRs have always been seen driven with aeroscreens, both on the race track and on the road. Indeed, Tony Jeanes, the owner of the red TR3A car on page 93 drives his car throughout the year on aeroscreens, no matter the weather. A true TR man!

Sun visors can be fitted, as shown in Fig 13.13. Here, tinted Perspex has been utilised, but 3mm acrylic sheet would do just as well.

13.13: Sun visor.

13.14: A 'wind-wing' attached to the screen frame can reduce buffeting.

13.15: An original Triumph factory aeroscreen. Factory ones differ from the aftermarket 'Brooklands' version by being taller and having a rubber seal at the bottom.

13.16: A 'Brooklands' type aeroscreen.

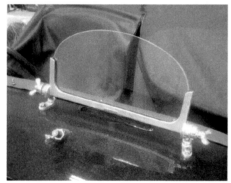

13.17: A TR3A sporting light blue metallic paintwork. While it might not be original it certainly looks good on the car.

Colours

Finally, one shouldn't forget about paint and trim colours. To cover all of the various options of TR trim that were available during the sidescreen cars' production run would take a book in itself.

However, one of the oddities that shows up from the factory records is that, despite the large number of cars that are sporting black leather or vinyl trim today, black was never an option on the TR2! The nearest shade to it was Blackberry, which was offered in the limited range of five paint colours available at the time. These were Ice Blue, Geranium Pink, Olive Yellow, Pearl White, and Black. There was no British Racing Green or Signal Red, both of which are very popular today.

Although up to eleven different colours were offered on the TR3A during its production run, by the time the last TR3A rolled off the line there were still only seven body colours to choose from. Ice Blue, Geranium Pink and Olive Yellow had long since been dropped, and they were eventually superseded by Salvador Blue, Silverstone Grey, and Pale Yellow.

13.18: This TR3A, owned by Tony Jeanes for over 50 years, is a well-known car in TR circles.

Today, a car that is being restored can be painted and trimmed to whatever suits your own personal preferences. The lines and curves of the TR2/3 can suit modern paint jobs, as Fig 13.17 shows, and the author knows of at least one TR2 that has been finished in solid two-tone red and white bodywork. Meanwhile the TR3 shown in Fig 13.19 uses grey and silver metallic paint to great effect.

That said, for resale value it's probably best to stick to the classic solid colours. Today, I think you would have to be rather brave to spray a car in gaudy Geranium Pink or bright

13.19: Two-tone paintwork is not to everyone's taste, but it works very well on this TR3.

Olive Yellow, but that's just a personal observation. It's worth remembering that Triumph, just like Porsche, Rolls-Royce and Bentley today, was only too happy to take your money, and would paint a car in whatever colour you liked.

14 Bodywork

14.1: A stripped down TR3A bodyshell undergoing restoration. The finished car is shown in the Introduction.

As stated in the introduction, the design of the bodyshell for the TR2 evolved from a design study that was carried out by Walter Belgrove for Sir John Black, the then Chairman of Standard Triumph.

The very first car was X505, the 20TS prototype. This carried most of the hallmarks of a TR2 from the front end up to the B-post, but, with its bobtail and exposed spare wheel, that's where any resemblance to a TR2 ended.

Fortunately, the redesigned longer chassis allowed for a more sloping tail and the enclosed spare wheel that we know today.

The new bodyshell sat on a separate but robust box girder chassis. The first five bodyshells were effectively handmade and they differ in various details from the actual production version that followed. Bodyshells were manufactured for Triumph at Mulliners of Birmingham, and then despatched to Coventry where they were 'married' to the rolling chassis on the final production line. Today, bodyshells are still said to be 'married' to their engines as they come down the production line.

Common problems

In the early 1950s rust protection in the motor industry was virtually non-existent. The TR's bodyshell wasn't immune to rust, but its saving grace was that immensely strong chassis. Unlike an MGB, which has a monocoque bodyshell, rust on a TR body doesn't affect the structural integrity of the chassis.

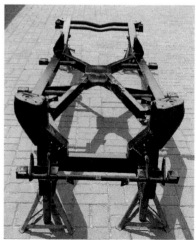

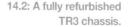

14.2: A fully refurbished TR3 chassis.

14.3: Replacing the boot floor on this TR2 is a big job, and can reveal a lot more tin worm underneath.

However, corrosion, accident damage and poor repairs can all take their toll on a bodyshell, and signs of this can be found by looking at the panel gaps around the bonnet, boot and doors in particular. Gaps should be consistent all round, with none being excessive. Doors should open evenly and shut flush with the rest of the bodywork. The alignment of the door crease with the front wing and rear quarter panel is a good indication of build and repair quality.

Bubbling paintwork is another sign that needs investigating, especially on the quarter panels, the edges of the tonneau panel, the bottom of the rear valance, the tops and edges of the rear wings, or around the rear of the front wings.

1 Misalignment

As the bodyshell sits on a separate chassis, all too often when a car is being restored the body is simply unbolted from the chassis and lifted off it so that remedial work can be carried out on the chassis. I say 'simply' because that is what the workshop manual would have you believe. In practice it can be a time-consuming process, but, once all the fixing nuts and bolts have been removed, four people can lift the body clear of the chassis. The process is made easier if the bodyshell has been strengthened with braces, as shown in Fig 14.4, before lifting it clear, but a badly rusted body will flex, and if the sills have gone there isn't much keeping the front and back halves together! For this reason it's important to have steel braces fitted between the A-post and the top of the rear wheelarch. You should also leave the doors on, and, if possible, bolt them to the braces as well before lifting the body clear of the chassis. On a long-door TR2, which only has inner sills, this bracing is especially important if you want to stop the body from folding in half.

Before we go on to discuss the body there's the chassis itself to consider. Accident damage, rust and poor repairs can seriously misalign a chassis and keep it out of square. A twisted chassis only has to be out by a few

14.4: Putting braces between the A- and B-posts is vital if you're to maintain bodyshell integrity during repairs.

14.5: With the bodyshell removed the chassis can be thoroughly inspected and stripped down to the last nut and bolt.

14.6: This TR3 chassis is showing severe signs of rust.

degrees for the body to become completely at odds with it, and no amount of packing will get the body to sit straight on the car afterwards.

The good news for TR2/3 owners is that the box girder chassis is immensely strong, and while it can suffer from rust it is rarely terminal. Check first for corrosion around the rear spring mountings, the two rear chassis cross tubes and the four outriggers for the body mountings. The

front half of the chassis hardly ever seems to suffer from rust.

Although not a cheap option, replacement chassis are available, so if your chassis is showing signs of accident damage, rust and/or poor repairs, then that might be a better long-term solution. Remember, TR2/3s are now over 60 years old – well past their original design lifespan, so think seriously about it, and, if in doubt, get a professional to do a drop check on the chassis to assess it for 'straightness and square.'

Body-wise, most misalignment of the panels comes about through poor sill replacement. Even if genuine 'Stanpart' panels are being used, a lot of these spares were said to be seconds from the production line, so a good fit was never guaranteed.

14.7: You can unbolt the whole of the front end. It's a big job but it makes getting the engine out a lot easier.

14.8: This shows a repair to the edge of the tonneau panel, which is a common rust spot.

Today's reproduction panels are very good, but will still need 'fettling' in order to achieve a good fit.

The replacement of sills, floorpans, inner wings and A- and

14.9: This is a post-TS60000 TR3A bodyshell, easily indentified by the flat rear floor. The rear quarter panel and the top of the inner rear wing are favourite spots for the rust bug. Note the 'top-hat' fixing for the hardtop.

14.10: This area around the boot is a real rust trap. The drain holes should be extended through the boot floor, but are often overlooked.

B-posts is not something to be undertaken lightly, and the complete body should be carefully assembled before final welding of the inner tub takes place. Try riveting or tack welding inner

14.11: With the front wing removed the A-post, inner sill and bulkhead can be examined for rust and repaired as necessary. The inner wing often rusts where it joins the bulkhead, and it's at this point you should address the problem of a lack of drainage.

body panels in place if you can, as this will help to ensure that the bolt-on outer panels will fit.

2 Rattles and squeaks

All TRs rattle to some extent, and my advice is to try and live with them. However, some rattles just shouldn't be there, so it's worth trying to trace those and fix them.

3 Doors and hinges

TR2/3 doors shouldn't rattle, but, if they do, it will probably be due to badly adjusted door locks. Checks should also be made for wear in the door hinges. If there's too much play they can produce an irritating squeak. Try oiling them first, but if that doesn't help then replacing the hinge pins should. One modification that can be made to the bonnet hinges is to press out the hinge pivots and replace them with removable ring pulls. While this is not a high priority modification, it's a useful mod if you're competing and you need to access the engine bay quickly.

The bonnet and boot lid hinges are made from Mazak, which is prone to pitting. On early cars they were always painted body colour, and they are handed so care must be taken to fit them correctly. Later cars, TR3 onwards, have chrome hinges. These can easily be replaced if necessary, but strangely, un-chromed hinges cost a lot more than chromed ones.

When hanging doors for an initial fit the hinges have a limited amount of adjustment on the A-post. However, if the door is already in place and you can lift the rear edge of the door then the hinges ought to be replaced as the hinge pins are worn.

It's a little known fact but there are two types of TR3A door. The later, post-TS60000 TR3As had all steel doors, whereas previously there was a wooden top rail. There was also a relatively minor change to the bottom rear edge of the door. They are curved on the inside but retain the square outer skin. However, if you do have to replace a door, do try to get the correct one.

If, when driving, you can see the gap between the door and the B-pillar opening and closing, then that's a sign of too much body flex. Check that all the alloy body mounting washers are still in place and correctly mounted. Some movement in the bodyshell is only to be expected, but if it seems excessive then it might be advisable to check the main body mountings and the chassis itself for damage and corrosion.

Finally, it pays to inspect the drainage tubes in the boot. The rubber pipes should pass through the floor, but are often missing or lack sealing. As this area is prone to rust it's worth checking. You can also add some extra rust protection by fitting proper drainage tubes behind the front wings, so that water from the bonnet can drain clear away rather than collect in the space behind the wing and closing panel.

4 Catches and locks

With today's cars being built with millimetre precision by robots we have come to expect car doors to close properly and with a satisfying 'clunk': just don't expect those on a 60 year old car to do the same! The door locks on the TR2/3 are fairly basic affairs, and could fly open in the event of an accident. A limited amount

14.12: Note the locking handle and the curved rear edge to the door on this photo of the author's TR3S.

of adjustment can be made on the B-post striker plate to make sure the doors shut properly. However, if the B-post has been replaced incorrectly then no amount of adjustment will make the door shut flush and line up with the rear quarter panel.

Neither the TR2 nor the TR3 was fitted with external door handles, relying instead on a pull cord accessed from inside the cabin, but the TR3A was. These were lockable and have integrated barrels operated by an FS series key. Reproduction door handles are now readily available.

The boot on the TR2 and TR3 had a key operated central boot lock, but there was no actual handle. They also sported two budget locks close to the rear corners of the boot, which were operated with a T-handle coach key. The chrome escutcheons for these should have spring-loaded 'tails' on them, but late TR3s and all 3As were fitted with the same circular ones as fitted to the spare wheel panel.

The boot on the TR3A dispensed with the budget locks and had a centre-mounted locking handle instead. Problems with the boot lock are rare, but it's a simple matter to replace it with a new one.

While on the subject of boot lids, pay attention to the rubber seal. There are various rubber cross sections available on the market, from a simple square shape to P-shaped profiles, which can offer a better seal against water ingress. However, whatever shape you go for it has to sit in a narrow channel around the edge of the boot opening.

The first 4000 or so TR2s had twin cable-operated bonnet locks (see Fig 14.14) operated from under the dashboard on the right-hand side of the footwell. The release cables have been known to fail, so it's a good idea to fit secondary emergency release cables to the bonnet lock levers and feed them down below the bulkhead where they can be easily accessed.

The majority of TR bonnets were fitted with Dzus fasteners, operated with the same T-handle key that is used for the boot, spare wheel cover and sidescreens.

The final lock, and one that is often overlooked, is that of the glovebox lid. It's common to all models, and requires careful adjustment of the striker plate if it's not to spring open after going over every bump in the road.

14.13: The rear end of a TR3A. The Triumph badge was never fitted to the TR2/TR3.

14.14: This close-up shows one of the two cable-operated internal bonnet locks on an early TR2.

Exterior fittings

The TR range, like many of its contemporaries, had various bits of trim to bring about some subtle differences between the various models. All of the cars feature a single blade chrome bumper to the front, with chrome overriders to the front and rear of the car. The rear overriders can sometimes be fitted upside down, so it's worth checking them. It's also worth noting that TR3A's bumper is of a different profile to the earlier cars, and has only two mounting irons instead of the earlier cars' four.

14.15: A TR2 front apron. Note the chrome trim around the mouth, and the starting handle mounting. The wing bead should be fabric-covered and not polished metal as shown here.

TR2s had fabric-covered wing beading, while TR3s and 3As had chrome wing beads fitted.

The grilles became the identifiable 'face' of the three models, with the TR2's being set back in the apron mouth, sometimes with (or without) a chrome moulding around the mouth. The TR3's 'egg box' grille is set at the front of the mouth, while the TR3A has a full-width 'dollar grin' grille set into a different front apron (see chapter 19 for detailed photos). Along with bonnet and boot hinges, all of these parts are now readily available from today's aftermarket suppliers.

The pressed alloy grille of the TR3A features combined indicators and sidelights at its ends. Some people, including TR2/3 owners, have converted the original white lenses to amber ones and fitted sidelights into the headlight units. While this might not be original, it's an attempt to make the cars a bit safer on today's roads.

14.16: The orange indicator lens on the front wing identifies this car as a TR3B. Export cars have to conform to different countries' rules on lighting, and this TR3B was built at the factory for a US customer who was serving in Germany.

All brightwork needs to be cared for, and regular washing and the application of a proprietary chrome cleaner like Solvol Autosol will help to keep the rust at bay.

Bumpers and overriders which are too far gone for re-chroming can now be replaced with stainless steel items. Wing mirrors were available in at least two designs. These could be fitted either to the tops of the wings above the wheelarches or could be fastened to the windscreen pillar. The author has never seen the point of fitting mirrors halfway down the wing, as you're

14.17: On this TR3A the owner has modified a windscreen Dzus fastener to accept a driving mirror. It's a very neat modification.

sitting too far away for them to be effective. It's much better to fit a mirror to the windscreen stanchion, as shown in Figure 14.17, where you can adjust it more easily.

The alloy stone guards fixed to the front of the rear wings are a two-part affair, and how they have been assembled gives you a clue as to how well any bodywork repairs have been carried out. As repro parts they don't always fit very well with repro wings, so a great deal of care needs to be taken when assembling the body if they are to fit correctly.

The only other bit of 'chrome' that needs mentioning is the windscreen assembly. The screen is removable by undoing the four Dzus fasteners that hold it in place. Removal is really a two man job, though, and on a standard car it cannot be stowed away. However, if you don't mind sacrificing a bit of bodywork to the closing side panels in the boot a screen can be slipped inside it. Removing the screen is advisable if you need to replace the glass. While this can be done at home, my advice is to let a specialist do it, as getting the new rubbers to seal properly can be difficult.

Looking after the body

Washing a car clear of accumulated road dirt is easy isn't it? You just need a bucket, lots of warm soapy water, a sponge, and a leather to dry it off afterwards. But is it really clean? Probably not. Cleaning the underside of the car will pay great dividends in terms of long-term ownership, so every so often it's a good idea to pressure wash the underside of the car to remove the build up of mud and debris that accumulates under the wheelarches and inside the front and rear wings. TRs send a lot of mud up into the rear wings, where it collects by the rear light housings, and this is a prime area for rust bubbles to start showing through. The same can be said of the front wings if the sealing plate between the inner and outer wings is missing. In short, if it's mud you are driving through, it will stick!

14.18: Fitting a drain pipe to the inner front wing box section is a very worthwhile modification.

If the car is only going to be used during the summer, then it's also a good idea at the end of the year to remove the seats and interior carpets to check on the condition of the floors and inner sills. This would also allow you to access the sills in order to spray some more Waxoyl inside them. While the Waxoyl is out, why not top up the chassis members at the same time?

The real key to a rust-free car is to undertake regular maintenance and to fix any blemishes before they develop into unsightly rust scars. The moral here is if you look after your car properly then it should look after you.

14.19 (above): When the paint has been removed it can reveal a host of horrors. Always check the condition of the sills and floors, especially if the carpet has been stuck down.

14.20 (top right): A US import might not be as described, so make sure you obtain good photographs before buying.

14.21 (right): A wheel spat as fitted to a TR2. These were an optional extra on TR2s, but can only be fitted on cars with steel wheels. They are a very rare sight today.

15 Infrequent use

While it's very unlikely that there are any owners today who could say that their TR2 is still their everyday car, quite a few cars are known to have been in long-term ownership for well over 30 years.

Having been relegated to being used only at weekends, many cars are now left in garages for weeks at a time without being used. Enforced idleness over the winter, too, does little to keep the car in tip-top condition, so it is a good idea to run the engine

15.2: A less radical approach is to fit a Dis-Car-Nect isolator to a battery terminal. Note also this very neat installation for the spare sparkplugs.

15.1: This racing TR has a key-operated battery isolator switch where the fuel gauge sat. The other red T-handle on top of the dash operates the fire extinguisher.

from time-to-time and move the car once in a while.

Cars that have been relegated to use on 'high days and holidays' or advertised for sale as DSUO (Dry Summer Use Only) are probably more susceptible to malfunctions than one that has been used on a regular basis.

So, if your car has been kept locked away in the garage waiting for the moment the sun starts to shine, then here are some tips to ensure that the next time you open the garage door the car will start and drive away happily.

The battery

Simply put, a battery that doesn't get used goes flat. Long periods of inactivity can destroy a battery if the charge in the cells falls below a certain level, so you really should invest in a trickle charger to keep the battery topped up. Fitting a battery isolator switch is also a good idea, because radios and clocks can still operate even if the ignition is switched off, and it will also prevent any short circuits.

Hydraulic fluid

Mineral-based clutch and brake fluid is hygroscopic, which means it absorbs moisture. Having water in either system is bad news, but, given the type of reservoir employed on all sidescreen TRs, you can guarantee that if water is in one system it will be in the other as well.

Of course the fluid should be changed at regular mileage intervals, but not having the car on the road all the year round means it can take years for those service intervals to come around.

If possible, replace the mineral-based fluid with a silicone one, but remember that the two types cannot be mixed, so drain and flush the system thoroughly.

The exhaust system

A standard mild steel system will corrode from the inside, even when not in use. There isn't much you can do about that so fit a stainless steel system (these usually have a lifetime guarantee). If you're going down that route it might be a good idea to change the manifold as well.

Brakes

If you are not going to use the car over the winter do not apply the handbrake. This will prevent the brake linings sticking to the rear drums. Needless to say, though, it's a good idea to chock the wheels. Before venturing out for the first time after a long period of inactivity check that the brakes are actually working (the rear wheel cylinders can develop a leak over time). If the car was put away wet, there'll probably be some build up of surface rust on the inside of the brake drums and on the surface of the front discs. As long as it's only a light covering then this will eventually clean off under braking. If it's more than that then scoring of the pads, linings and the discs or drums can occur. Don't be surprised to hear a lot of brake squeal as you drive off for the first time after a long winter lay-up.

The clutch

If the car isn't going to be used for some months then it's advisable to keep the clutch pedal depressed, as it's not unknown for the clutch plate to seize onto the flywheel. If that has happened, the remedy is as follows: chock the wheels, select top gear, apply the handbrake fully, press the clutch, and then operate the starter. The torque from the starter motor should be enough to free the plate, but if more than a few attempts are required and it still doesn't come free then it might require the removal of the gearbox to free it. One way to prevent the clutch sticking is to keep it depressed by putting a suitably sized piece of wood between the pedal and the dashboard.

The engine

If possible do try to run the engine up to operating temperature every fortnight, but if that's just not possible then it should be once a month as an absolute minimum. If the car is going into long-term storage then it's a very good idea to drain all the oil and water from the engine – not forgetting the oil filter and the oil cooler if fitted. That way any contaminants will be flushed out of the engine. You can replenish the cooling system with distilled water and the engine with some cheap but fresh oil. It's also a very good idea to remove the sparkplugs and squirt some engine oil into the cylinders. DO NOT fill them up, though, as you risk hydraulic locking of the engine if you forget about it and then try starting the engine. It's best to put a reminder notice on the steering wheel of the car if you do. Again, with the sparkplugs removed, it's also advisable to turn the engine over BY HAND to ensure it will turn over freely. With the plugs still removed you can then operate the starter motor in order to pump some oil around the engine.

The fuel system

Whether you have an original mechanical fuel pump or a replacement electric one it's worth starting the car once in a while to make sure it's working okay. Try not to leave too much fuel in the tank if leaving the car for long periods, as petrol loses its 'lights' and goes stale. I always try to add a fresh gallon or two if possible to help with the volatility of the fuel.

Tyres

Prolonged lack of use over the winter can cause tyres to develop 'flat spots' where they are in contact with the floor of the garage. Avoid this by moving the car so that the tyres don't sit in the same position all the time. Better still, jack up the car onto axle stands, remove the wheels completely and stack them flat. Also remember that tyres harden with age and deteriorate, so while a tyre might look good and have plenty of tread left on it, it could actually be a hazard, so do check that date stamp that is found on every tyre.

And finally

Before setting off on your first trip of the year, make sure that everything is working as it should. That means checking the electrics, wipers, indicators, etc, and waiting for the engine to get up to working oil pressure and temperature. A bit of patience here can save you both time and money.

15.3: The 3308 on this tyre means it was made in August (week 33) of 2008, and for safety's sake it should now be replaced.

16 Competition & modifications

16.1: The author's much-modified racing TR3S.

16.2: VHP 529, one of the original Apple Green works rally cars from 1958, still being rallied around Europe by Iain Paul.

From the very outset, competition had been at the heart of the TR range of sports cars. In 1954, not long after the TR2 entered production, one car, OKV 777, was entered into the prestigious 24-hour Le Mans race where it finished in a very creditable 15th place. In the same year another TR2 won the RAC Rally, so its sporting credentials were first class right from the very beginning. The TR2/3 owner can, therefore, look back and reflect upon a very good competition heritage.

Before international rallying moved into the forest stages, a sidescreen TR really was THE car to have for rallying. These cars achieved great success in the Alpine Rally, winning prizes right through from 1954 to 1960. In international racing it was much the same, with the works cars entering Le Mans, the Mille Miglia and the Sebring 12 hours. Consequently, the TR became very popular with SCCA racing in the USA, and many drivers, including future World Champion Phil Hill, cut their racing teeth driving a TR2/3.

The growth of historic racing in recent years has seen a resurgence in TRs of all types competing on the track and in rallying. A number of specialist firms now cater for the motorsports enthusiast, and engines can now easily produce 200bhp, which is more than double what the factory offered in 1955! Meanwhile, the aftermarket sector has produced a whole

16.3: This immaculate TR2 belongs to Richard Owen, who is a regular class-winning competitor in historic racing.

16.4: The author's view from the seat of a TR3A on the Land's End trial. And, yes, that is a TR7 we're catching up!

host of goodies that an owner can fit to personalise their car.

In the 1970s and '80s the TR Register car club did a great deal to promote competition by organising sprints and its own race championship. Today there is the Revington Sprint and Hillclimb Championship, and TRs have also begun to make their mark in Equipe GTS and the HSCC series.

Make no mistake about it, though, going racing isn't cheap, and even if it's only sprints and hillclimbs you decide to enter, your wallet will still take a pounding. Also, it's worth noting that while your road car can be made to go faster, if you want it to be competitive then it will no longer really be suitable for you to pop down to the pub in, so think carefully before you commit yourself to preparing the car for the track!

Some basics

Modifying the engine is only part of the story, but it's often the one that people make the mistake of spending money on first. My simple advice is DON'T! Even on a road car, if you want to go faster then the first things you should be paying attention to are the brakes. The reason for this is because if you can brake later into a corner then you will be the first one out of it. After that it's the suspension that needs looking at in order to make the car handle better. Remember, it's not top speed that counts on a race track, but rather how you can put down the power and get through the corners that makes the difference.

Safety is all important, so a proper roll cage, harness and protective clothing are all required before starting your competition journey.

1 Think before you modify

Replacing worn out parts like shock absorbers and suspension bushes will often transform a car from a stodgy one that lurches around corners into a much crisper motoring experience.

Similarly, if your HT leads are old and cracked then fit some new ones, and, while you're at it, think about replacing the distributor with an electronic one if the regulations allow. If that's all that you require from your car then so be it, but if you want to turn it into more of a fire breathing monster that can keep up with today's traffic (remember, even a Skoda Citigo can do 100mph!) then you'll need to think

16.6: The TR3S owned by the author is fitted with the very rare DU6 twin-choke SU racing carbs, but it is still useable on the road.

seriously about how you're going to boost the car's performance. However, before doing anything, set yourself a realistic budget and time-frame within which to complete the work. The author knows of several cars that were once quite roadworthy examples but have now been off the road for several years simply because the bar was set too high, the money ran out, and life got in the way.

2 Reliability

Boosting a car's performance will have an impact on the car's reliability. Highly tuned engines are a pain to keep in tune, and, while 180-200bhp is now attainable from a TR2/3, ask yourself if it's worth it, and where are you going to use it? 150bhp will be just as good on a fast road car, and the car will be more reliable to boot. Fitting a modern five-speed gearbox in place of the standard four-speed plus overdrive one might be just the ticket. There will no longer be electrical connections to break down – which they do – and the gear ratios will be better. Purists might be offended, but power steering and mapped ignition systems are now readily available on the aftermarket. While such mods might not be original, if they make the car more pleasant to drive then why not fit them? They can always be removed later if so desired.

16.7: Another highly modified TR3, but this time fitted with more modern 45DCOE Weber carbs.

3 Servicing

The more you change from the original specification, the more you will pay for a service, either at your local garage or with one of the TR specialists around the country. Mechanics will have to tune and/or replace parts specific to your car, and they might not be readily available, especially if they come from a competing supplier!

4 Safety

Okay, so now you have 200bhp under the bonnet and your car will do 130mph. That's great, but your TR2 is still on its original drum brakes! Well that's a shame because the next time you try to stop may see you end up in the graveyard! You cannot expect 60-year-old brakes to stop a car with 35 per cent more power. If you do upgrade the engine power then you must improve the stopping ability. Follow what Triumph did and fit discs and callipers first before looking at the engine mods.

16.8: This TR3 has original discs and callipers, but they could be upgraded to vented discs and modern four-pot callipers.

16.9: The rear brakes can also be improved by fitting 'Alfin' style drums. Note also the rear anti-roll bar and adjustable shock absorber.

Evolutionary modifications

Not everyone wants to be on the race track, but they do want to modify their car with sensible upgrades that will impart some pride of ownership.

These items fall into two distinct categories: those that can improve the mechanical side of the car; and others which are purely visual. Taking the mechanical side first, this would include fitting copper brake pipe and braided stainless steel hoses, changing the rear crank seal, or fitting Weber carbs or an oil

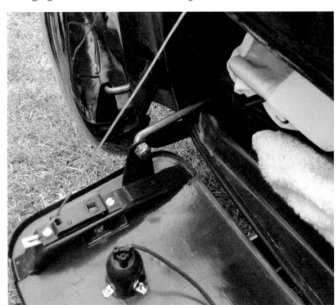

16.10: Not all mods come from the factory. This enterprising owner has fitted a unique sliding hinge to the spare wheel access panel.

cooler, etc. On the cosmetic side it could be new seats and trim, a Moto-Lita type steering wheel, or a set of chrome wire wheels. The list is long and new products are being released all the time. The only limiting factor is the size of your wallet.

In period, Triumph offered quite a number of accessories to help owners modify their TR2/3, ranging from competition springs and sump guards to more mundane items like badge bars, cigarette lighters and boot racks.

Modifying for competition

First of all decide what level of competition you want to enter. The build spec for a sprint car will be very different from that of a race car, and even more so if you want to go rallying. The next step is to get hold of the regulations for the type of event

16.13: A full race TR engine being prepared for installation. Note the four-branch manifold, alloy cylinder head, and other lightweight components.

16.11: This TR3A owner has opted for Mazda MX5 seats, chrome wire wheels, a boot rack and a roll over bar for safety.

16.12: The ingenious owner of this TR3A has utilised the wasted space underneath the rear seat to incorporate two hidden lockers, deep enough to hold a spare petrol can, tools, or even a laptop.

you're interested in. These will tell you what is and what is not allowed, and should be read in conjunction with the RAC/MSA *Blue Book* of motorsport regulations, and in particular Appendix K. You will also need to apply for your competition licence and join an MSA recognised club. By doing so you'll be able to tap into the existing members' knowledge, thus saving you a lot of money, and they will be only too happy to welcome you into the club.

The author started his competition 'career' by sprinting his everyday TR5. As it was a daily driver, attention was paid to make the engine produce the best of its available horsepower by carefully balancing all of the rotating parts, pistons and rods.

16.14: The Judson supercharger on this TR2 was a popular period modification, but is quite rare today.

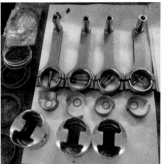

16.16: A set of high-performance conrods and pistons: not cheap, but bulletproof!

16.17: Steel hubs on the left for strength, alloy hubs on the right for lightness.

The result was a smoothly revving engine that could happily exceed the originally designed rev limit.

So what can be done to a TR2/3? The latest cars can have fully mapped ignition systems, ceramic coated exhausts, steel nitrided crankshafts, lightweight alloy hubs and radiators. There are also dog boxes, adjustable

16.15: An even rarer supercharger is this Arnott 'blower.'

suspension and limited slip differentials, plus a host of other modifications, are available from TR specialists like TR Enterprises, Revington TR and Racetorations, the owners of which have all competed with great success over the years in both rallying and circuit racing.

Rolling roads

Whether it be a race car or a fast road car, your TR will benefit from having a session on a rolling road. Even if you have only modified the inlet and exhaust ports, a rolling road test will show you where the power is coming from, and may even improve your economy. On cars fitted with much hotter cams and electronic ignition it's a false economy not to go onto a rolling road, because no amount of spanner work will adjust your car as accurately as the computer can.

A rolling road measures the amount of torque being generated at a particular engine speed (rpm) and when divided by 5.252

16.18: The author takes a break while competing on the Land's End Trial in Phil Tucker's highly modified TR3A.

Weight Saving Fibre-Glass Body Parts
FOR THE TR2, 3 and 3A

FRONT APRONS (TR3A Style, long-grill) Weight saving of appx. 14 lbs.

FRONT WINGS in Fibreglass Weight saving of appx. 10 lbs. per wing.

You may therefore bring your older Model TR2 up to date (and save weight) by fitting one of these modern style TR3A Front Aprons.

S.A.H. ACCESSORIES
THE TR2/3 SPECIALISTS
VIMY DRIVE, LEIGHTON BUZZARD, BEDS.
Tel.: Leighton Buzzard 3022.

16.19: An SAH advert dating from 1959 extolling the virtues of fitting fibreglass panels to your TR. Many are still available today.

it gives the amount of horsepower (bhp) at the back wheels for those revs. The difference between the two is that bhp tells you how fast you were going when you hit a tree while torque tells you how far you moved it!

Adding lightness

The late, great Colin Chapman of Lotus Cars is reported to have said "If you want to win then add lightness." A lot of light alloy mechanical components for TR2/3s ranging from hubs to cylinder heads are now available, but the ultimate must be the handcrafted alloy bodyshells from North Devon Metal Craft. However, if aluminium panels are beyond your reach, many fibreglass panels are still available. Indeed there were many TR2s and TR3s in the 1950s that had their front aprons swapped for a fibreglass TR3A one. It was a relatively cheap way to update the look of one's car.

Finally, competition is about having fun in your TR, and there can be no better challenge than to take part in one of the many retrospective rallies that are held, such as Le Jog, the Mille Miglia, and, of course, the iconic Monte Carlo Rally.

16.20: A new fibreglass front apron for a TR3A. Much cheaper than a secondhand steel one, even today!

16.21: A tricky moment for a TR, on full opposite lock, captured at night on the Monte Carlo retrospective rally.

Probably the best tool ever been invented for the classic car owner is the mobile phone. Unless you're very unlucky or a Luddite you no longer have to walk along the motorway hard shoulder to get to an emergency phone box. Help is at hand with a phone call to your preferred roadside assistance company ... or is it? The author's own experience is coloured by the fact that on the two occasions when his TRs did break down, neither the AA nor the RAC could fix the cars. The first 'mechanic' had never even seen a carburettor before, and the other couldn't believe there wasn't a 'black box' available on the car to plug his laptop into. Such is the world of classic car motoring in the modern age!

With these sorry tales in mind, it is, therefore, useful to carry a small assortment of spares and tools with you. A circular biscuit tin, for example, can fit snugly into the spare wheel, and the space around it can carry all sorts of useful items. Originally, the TR2/3 did come with a pillar jack operated from inside the car after removing one of the rubber bungs in the floorpan, just ahead of the seats. However, this raised both wheels on one side off the ground, which isn't really necessary. Today, many owners use a scissor-type jack and wheel brace for changing the wheel, but some prefer to use a small bottle jack instead. The author doesn't recommend this, though, as getting a bottle jack under the front of the chassis on a car with a flat tyre is almost impossible.

Cars fitted with wire wheels as standard came with a copper headed hammer in order to undo them. Other tools that could be supplied with the car were two tyre levers, two box spanners, three open-ended spanners, an adjustable wrench, a flat-bladed screw driver (no Phillips screws back then) a grease gun, and some pliers. While some people like to display an original tool roll, the author's opinion is that you are better off with a much more modern tool kit!

What to carry with you

With just a very few exceptions, all of the nuts and bolts on a TR2/3 are AF, so don't bother with that nice shiny tool box with a wide selection of metric sockets and spanners in it. Tool kit

17.1: A collection of spares you should keep in your car.

17.2: A selection of spanners, screwdrivers and pliers can come in handy, but cable ties and duct tape are essential items.

It's a good idea to carry a spare set of bulbs, especially if you ever intend to go touring in Europe.

Other electrical items worth carrying are a spare HT coil (you can fit it to the inner wing, which keeps it handy) and a set of sparkplugs (see Fig 15.2 for a neat storage solution). Include if you can a spare distributor cap, rotor arm, points and a condenser. In addition, a thermostat and some gasket sealant would also be useful, but carrying things like clutch plates and brake pads is frankly a waste of valuable space. Such things should be attended to BEFORE you set out on your journey. Most of the suggested items can be put into a round tin and placed inside the spare wheel to save space.

Some form of torch (perhaps a head torch) is a useful addition to any tool kit, and a spare bottle of water can help with any overheating problems. Jump leads can be useful too, but there are now compact devices on the market that can start your car and seem to have enough power to kill an elephant. If all else fails, pack a tow rope! Finally, a workshop manual would be a very useful item to have on board.

Back at home

Classic car owners are well known for collecting tools and spares that one day may or may not get used, but what does the average enthusiast really need in his garage?

First of all the aforementioned workshop manual is a must. After that a decent trolley jack and axle stands will get your car up in the air ready for you to take off its wheels so you can get at it, under it and inside it. A decent spring compressor is a good investment if you're going to strip the suspension, but you can make one yourself with some ½in high tensile threaded rod, a few nuts, and a bit of ¼in steel or thick alloy plate. Another good set of spanners, sockets and screwdrivers specifically for the garage

essentials for me are combination open end/ring spanners in sizes from ¼in up to 1in AF, and the same in sockets, with a ⅜in drive. Mole (vise) grips, a Stanley knife with spare blades, a junior hacksaw, and a variety of flat-bladed and cross-headed screwdrivers of different lengths. A hammer, some electrical wire, crimps and connectors, spare fuses, tie tags, and that essential roll of duct tape are also all sensible things to carry with you.

Spares-wise you should carry a fanbelt, some jubilee clips (hose clamps), a set of radiator hoses, and, if possible, a water pump, as a pump failure is the most likely breakdown you can fix at the side of the road yourself without being towed to a garage.

17.3: A decent spring compressor like this can make a job so much easier.

are next – don't use the in-car set, as you will leave them on a bench and forget to put them back.

Other, more specialist items, like torque wrenches, compression testers, air tools, and timing lights are all very useful, but only if a) you know how to use them, and b) you actually do your own servicing. With air compressors being available for £100 or less, it's a good idea to have one (them make maintaining tyre pressures easy). A lot of modern cars now carry small 12-volt air pumps, and these can be a good buy. As for other tools, such as arc welders and blasting cabinets, ask yourself, are they really necessary?

Spare parts

The TR2/3 owner today is very well catered for, with a huge range of spare parts available from the various specialist suppliers. You can buy a brand new chassis, and most mechanical parts are available, too. Cast iron and alloy cylinder heads have been remanufactured by Moss, with the help of the TR Register and the TR Spares Development Fund. The TR Spares Development Fund is now an independent not-for-profit body whose sole interest is to help keep TRs on the road. To this end it purchases original panels and parts to use as patterns to enable items that are no longer available to be remanufactured. Examples of which are the TR2 thermostat housing and the chrome TR3 grille moulding.

However, while the big shiny bits are readily available, all too often it's that little bit of trim that's no longer supplied. This is where membership of one of the TRSDF and various TR car clubs comes in useful, because while the dealers might not have the part you are looking for you can bet someone else does. The other good places to look for spares are at the various classic auto jumbles that take place.

17.4: A good trolley jack, axle stands, a compressor and a sturdy tool cabinet are all worthwhile purchases for the home garage.

17.5: Buying a used gearbox can be fraught with problems if you don't know what you are looking for. The author has always got Peter Cox to build his gearboxes for both road and racing use, but there are several other specialists who can do the same.

When replacing a part on your car do check that it's the right one, and if it's a repro part make sure it's of good quality. Many repro parts are a bit dubious in this respect, rotor arms being one of the more notorious items for failing. Wheel bearings, too, can be very suspect if you opt for the cheapest on the market. If in doubt buy the best, which in this case are Timken bearings.

Overall, it's a false economy to buy really cheap parts. It's worth spending some time tracking down original old stock or even good secondhand parts rather than using repro versions.

18 The TR community

With limited spares support from the factory early TR models were fast disappearing from our roads. In the autumn of 1969 the magazine *MotorSport* published a series of letters on the topic of 'what makes a sports car.' Several readers said that a TR2/3 was a really good sports car that was cheap to buy and offered 100mph performance with reasonable economy. At the time a roadworthy TR could be bought for £200 so they were perfect for impoverished enthusiasts who couldn't afford a new car.

UK clubs

Today there are a number of clubs worldwide that can offer a home and advice for TR2/3 owners.

The TR Register

The first of these clubs was the TR Register, formed on January 11th 1970 at Hopcroft's Holt, Steeple Aston, Oxfordshire.

Initially, the club catered only for sidescreen cars, but long before Triumph became a footnote in history, the 'windy window' TRs also became eligible for membership. The TR Register is now one of the largest one-make car clubs in the UK and has around 6000 members in total. The club has 56 local UK groups and 23 affiliated overseas ones in Europe, South Africa and as far away as Japan, Australia and New Zealand. It produces the award winning all-colour magazine *TRACTION*, promotes competition, track days, overseas tours, and hosts a three-day International Weekend every year. Its office can be found at:

TR Register, 1B Hawksworth, Southmead Industrial Park, Didcot,

18.1: The TR Register owns the very first RHD TR2. Members are encouraged to drive it, and here Chris Barrie of *Red Dwarf* fame, a TR owner himself, takes it for a spin.

Oxon, OX11 7HR. Tel: +44 (0) 1235 818866.
Website: www.tr-register.co.uk. Email: office@tr-register.co.uk

The TR Drivers Club

Founded in 1981, it originally aimed to cater for the later TR7 and TR8 cars, but now caters for all models of TR. Today, Chris Turner is its enthusiastic Chairman, and he's supported by a network of volunteers. The club can be contacted via info@trdrivers.com, and I'm pleased to say that both clubs now work together for the benefit of all their members.

The TSOA (UK)

The Triumph Sports Owners Association was originally formed in 1953 by the factory, but it fell by the wayside when Triumph was absorbed in the British Leyland empire. While there are still branches in the USA and Australia, it has recently been revived here in the UK. Aimed at, as the name suggests, the more sporting owner, it encourages its members to use their cars more by hosting a number of meetings and events at selected venues around the country. While primarily focused on the sidescreen TRs it also welcomes members with later TR models and other sporting Triumphs.

Website: www.tosa.co.uk. Email: info@tsoa.co.uk.

The Triumph Sports Six Club (TSSC)
As its name suggests the club was formed to cater primarily for the six-cylinder Triumph models (TR6, GT6 and Vitesse), but it also embraces Spitfire and Herald derivatives. It has a suite of offices in Lubenham, Leicester, where members can buy spares, get a coffee, and see some of the historic cars it has on display there. The address is:

Sunderland Court, Main Street, Lubenham, Leicestershire, LE16 9TF. Tel: +44 (0)1858 434424. Fax: +44 (0)1858 431936. Email: info@tssc.org.uk

Club Triumph
Club Triumph is the oldest Triumph club for all models, having been formed in 1961. The club, run by volunteers, provides maximum opportunity for members to drive their cars, from social runs organised by one of over 20 local groups, to longer runs, autosolos and 12 car rallies. The Club's biennial Round Britain Reliability Run, first run in 1966, now attracts over 120 crews, and, since 1990, has raised over three quarters of a million pounds for many deserving charities. The RBRR alternates with the Ten Countries Run, a five-day tour of Europe incorporating Alpine passes and other great driving roads. Members receive a full colour A4 magazine, *Club Torque*, six times a year.Website: www. club.triumph.org.uk. Email: enquiries@club.triumph.org.uk

Standard Triumph sports cars were exported all over the world and overseas production facilities were set up to assemble some models from what were known as CKD (Completely Knocked Down) kits. As a result, there are strong club followings in several countries around the globe, with America being home to a number of Triumph clubs.

TR Clubs in the USA
There are several clubs in the USA that cater for the TR2/3/3A/3B owner, first and foremost of these is the Vintage Triumph Register or VTR as it is sometimes known.

Vintage Triumph Register (VTR)
Tracing its roots back to 1973, the VTR caters for Triumph enthusiasts in the USA and Canada, and covers the diverse range of Standard Triumph cars, from the prewar Triumph Southern Cross, through the later saloons such as the Mayflower and Standard 10, right up to the TR8. As a result, the club has over 2700 members spread all across America and in affiliated groups. The club can be contacted via its website: www. vintagetriumphregister.org

18.2: This American TR3A meets up with its eventual successor, the TR4.

Buckeye Triumphs of America

Formed in 1998, this group is one of those affiliated to the VTR above. This site offers a wealth of helpful technical information, and can be contacted via its website: www.buckeyetriumphs.org

Connecticut Triumph Register

This appears to be an independent Triumph TR club that holds a variety of meetings to the North East of New York. Contact via the website: www.conntriumph@gmail.com

Detroit Triumph Sports Car Club

This is an offshoot of the VTR based as its name implies near the city of Detroit. Members meet at Brass Pointe Restaurant in Farmington Hills. Website: www.detroittriumph.org

Georgia Triumph Association

Another VTR affiliated club based near Atlanta. Website: http://www.gatriumph.com

Portland Triumph Owners Association

This covers the Portland, Oregon, Washington State and Vancouver areas. Contact via the website: www.portlandtriumph.org

Triumph Sports Car Club of San Diego

Based in sunny California, this is one of the smaller Triumph clubs in America but has an enthusiastic social following from its 120 or so members. Contact via the website: www.sandiegotriumphclub.com

Triumph Travelers Sports Car Club

This is another club affiliated to the VTR of America, and organises events for west coast Triumph enthusiasts. Contact Triumph Travelers Sports Car Club, Box 60314, Sunnyvale, California CA94088-0314. Website: www.triumphtravelers.org

Triumph Club of Southern California

This was originally formed in 1979 and caters for a wide variety of Triumph sports cars of all ages. Contact via the website: www.sctoa.org

TR clubs in Australia
Triumph Car Club of the ACT (Canberra)

Website: https://allancaldwell1.wixsite.com/act-triumph-car-club. Email: acttriumphcarclub@gmail.com

Triumph Car Club of Victoria

Website: https://www.tccv.net

Triumph Car Club of Western Australia (Perth)

Website: www.tccwa.com

Triumph Sporting Owners Association (Victoria)

This is an offshoot of the UK TSOA, which was formed in Britain in 1953. Contact The Secretary, PO Box 5020Y, Melbourne, Victoria. 3001 Website: www.tsoavic.com.au

New Zealand
The TR club of New Zealand

This is a very active club, which the author has had the pleasure of visiting. Contact Frank Cleary, who owns one of the very rare Dove GTR4s. The club hosts its very own 'International' Rally, which attracts visitors from Australia and the UK. Website: www.trregister.org.nz. Email: info@trregister.co.nz

Manufacturer's production records and archive

British Motor Industry Heritage Trust, Heritage Motor Centre, Banbury Road, Gaydon, Warwickshire. CV35 0BJ. Tel: 01926 641188. Website: www.heritage-motor-centre.co.uk

UK main spares suppliers

British Motor Heritage Ltd
Range Road, Cotswold Business Park, Witney, OX29 0YB. Tel: +44 (0) 1993 707200. Website: www.bmh-ltd.com.

Moss-Europe
Hampton Farm Estate, Hanworth, Middlesex, TW9 6DB. Tel: +44 (0) 20 8867 2020. Website: www.moss-europe.co.uk. Email: sales@moss-europe.co.uk. Branches in London, Bradford, Bristol, Manchester and Paris.

18.3: This is a later TR2 exported to its new home in New Zealand.

Rimmer Brothers
Triumph House, Sleaford Road, Bracebridge Heath, Lincoln, LN4 2NA. Tel: +44 (0) 1522 568000. Website: www.rimmerbros.co.uk. Email: sales@rimmerbros.co.uk.

TR Bitz
Appleton Autodrome, Swineyard Lane, High Legh, Knutsford, Cheshire, WA16 0SD. Tel +44 (0) 1925 756000. Website: www.trbitz.com. Email: info@trbitz.com.

Revington TR
Thorngrove Barns, 10 Main Road, Middlezoy, Bridgwater, TA7 0PD. Tel: +44 (0) 1823 698437. Website: www.revingtontr.com. Email: info@revingtontr.com.

TR Enterprises
Dale Lane, Blidworth, Mansfield, Nottingham, NG21 0TG. Tel: +44 (0) 1623 793807. Website: www.trenterprises.com. Email:info@trenterprises.com.

TRGB
Unit 1 Sycamore Farm Industrial Estate, Long Drove, Somersham, Huntingdon, Cambridgeshire, PE28 3HJ. Tel: +44 (0) 1487 842168. Website: www.trgb.co.uk. Email: sales@trgb.co.uk.

Protek Engineering
Unit 13 Bushells Business Estate, Wallingford, Oxon. Tel: +44 (0) 1491 832372.

Robsport
Unit 1-3 North End, Dunsbridge Turnpike, Shepreth, Royston,

SG8 6RA. Tel: +44 (0) 1763 262263. Website: www.robsport.co.uk.

David Manners Group
991 Wolverhampton Road, Oldbury, West Midlands, B69 4RJ. Tel: +44 (0) 121 544 4040. Website: www.davidmanners.co.uk. Email: enquiries@davidmanners.co.uk.

Prestige Developments & Injection
Tel: +44 (0) 1978 263449. Website: www.prestigeinjection.net.

Peter Cox & Son Sports Cars
Unit 25 Peltland Trading Estate, Padgets Lane, Redditich, B98 0RB. Tel: +44 (0) 1527 552646. Website: www.petecoxsportscars.co.uk. Email: enquiry@petecoxsportscars.co.uk.

The Distributor Doctor
Unit 8, Old Brewery Road. Wiveliscombe, Taunton, TA4 2PW. Tel: 01984 629540. Website: www.distributordoctor.com. Email: martin@distributordoctor.com.

CTM Engineering Ltd (TR Chassis specialist)
Tel: +44 (0) 7388 729129. Website: www.ctmengineering.co.uk. Email: colin@ctmengineering.co.uk.

TR Spares Development Fund (TRSDF)
Website: www.info@TRSDF.co.uk

USA spares suppliers
The Roadster Factory
328 Killen Road, Armagh, Pennsylvania, USA. Tel: 001 (800) 283-3723. Website: www.the-roadster-factory.com. Email: trfmail@trfmail.com.

Other useful forums
https://www.tr-register.co.uk/forums
www.sideways-technologies.co.uk

Finally, if you want even more TR ephemera in your home there are plenty of models out there for you to collect.

19.1: The grille at the back of the air intake helps to identify this car as a TR2.

19.2: Even without its front bumper, the forward-mounted 'egg crate' grille identifies this car as a TR3.

With a production run lasting from 1953 to 1962, it is only to be expected that there were a number of revisions made right through TR2-3B production. The majority of these were made to the TR2, with some 47 major and minor changes being made through its three-year production run. They include such major items as replacing the long doors with short doors to clear

kerbs when parking, to minor ones like fitting a rubber cover on the overdrive solenoid. However, for the TR3A owner, possibly the biggest option was a choice of engine size.

Starting with the TR2, the TS series engine had an 83mm x 92mm bore and stroke, which gave it a capacity of 1991cc with a compression ratio of 8.5 to 1. Power was stated as

19.3: The full-width grille identifies this car as a TR3A. Note the front apron has a less bulbous profile, too.

19.4: The engine number is stamped into the block (arrowed) and should be clearly legible.

being 90bhp at 4800rpm, while maximum torque was 117lbft at 3000rpm. However, when the TR3A came along with the larger 2138cc (86mm x 92mm bore and stroke) it was still possible to order the car with the smaller 1991cc engine as an option.

When the TR3B was introduced in 1962 for the American market, the first 500 cars were given TSF commission numbers.

However, for the rest of the TR3B production run commission numbers changed to TCF prefixes. The reason for this is that while they were visually identical to each other, the later cars were fitted with 2138cc TR4 engines and all synchromesh gearboxes. As such, an American TCF series TR3B is highly sought after.

Engines have numbers stamped into the block, as shown in Fig 19.4. While they are not an exact match for a car's commission number, they can be very close and, in today's market, cars are often advertised as having 'matching numbers' showing it still has its original engine or gearbox fitted. This can often attract a higher premium when it comes to a sale.

While the gearbox ratios remained the same throughout the production life of sidescreen TRs, from 1957 the final drive units were offered with a choice of ratio. Cars were fitted with a 3.7:1 axle ratio as standard, but the 4.1:1 ratio could be ordered if the car was fitted with overdrive. Incidentally, an 'O' at the end of the commission number indicates that the car was fitted with overdrive at the factory. It's worth noting that cars with overdrive but without this letter 'O' on the commission plate have been retrofitted.

The top speed of the 1991cc TR2 was reported to be 103mph, which was marginally higher than the TR3's recorded 102mph! Similarly, fuel consumption was recorded as being 5mpg better than that of the TR3 at 33mpg, but the author's own experience of driving his TR2 fitted with overdrive showed that 40+mpg could easily be attained on a long run.

How to identify a car?

The commission plate denoting which car you're looking at is found on the bulkhead. The first production TR2 was TS1 LO, a LHD car that was exported to Canada, while TS2 was the first RHD car and was shipped to Dublin. Amazingly, both of these cars still exist: TS1 is in America, while TS2 was generously donated to the TR Register by its long-term owner Keith Read, and is used to promote the Club's activities.

The first five cars were prototypes and were accordingly issued 'X' numbers by the factory. X519 was the second prototype, and it was this LHD car that was sent to Belgium to attempt the speed record for under 2-litre sports cars. Registered MVC 575, it broke the record by topping 124mph

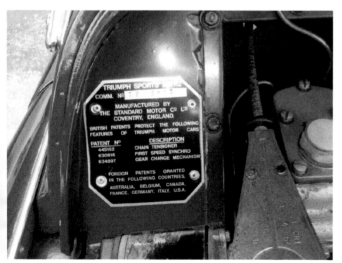

19.5: A commission plate on a TR2.

19.6: The commission plate on a TR3A.

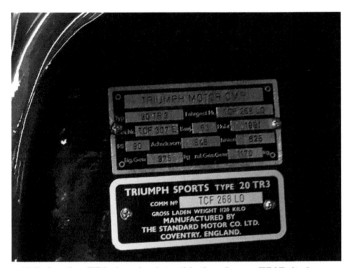

19.7: Another TR3 chassis plate, this time from a TR3B. It shows the car is LHD and fitted with overdrive, while the upper plate says it has a 1991cc engine. A rare car indeed as only 530 were fitted with this engine.

19.8: The brass plates on the bulkhead are body numbers and should not be confused with commission numbers.

as an average of two runs over a measured mile in opposite directions. It has recently undergone a painstaking restoration by Glen Hewitt of Protek Ltd. The car is now on permanent display at the British Motor Museum, Gaydon, thanks to a Heritage Memorial Fund Lottery grant, but it would have been scrapped years ago had it not been rescued by Mr John Ames, who had the foresight to save it from destruction.

With the exception of the TR3B, which had TSF or TCF commission numbers, all USA cars carried the same TS identification prefix on the chassis plate. However, cars built in Belgium from kits supplied by the factory had the letter 'N' added as a suffix to the commission number.

UK and rest of the world production

Altogether Triumph built 8628 TR2s, a further 13,377 TR3s, 58,236 TR3As, and 3331 TR3Bs, making a total production run of 83,572 cars. This was nearly 15,000 more cars than the subsequent models that replaced them, the TR4/4A.

Needless to say the majority of these early TRs went to the USA and elsewhere in the world. In fact only 6005 sidescreen

19.9: The Triumph brand might have disappeared, but classic racing helps to keep TRs in the public eye.

19.10: Tony Dron, the last 'works' driver for Triumph, and Nick Marsh compete at Classic Le Mans 2005. Note also the Standard Vanguard team support car.

cars were sold in the UK, which made them a pretty rare sight in postwar Britain, and all the more desirable for that. While there might not be that many on our roads now, the survival rate in the UK is pretty good.

A decent TR2/3/3A can still be bought for reasonable money, although good condition cars are now changing hands for around £28k+, while a few exceptional cars can command even higher prices. It seems that originality is the key to obtaining top money for road-going cars, while cars like the ex-works Le Mans TR2 shown in Fig 19.9, or rally cars that have a proven competition history, have recently fetched six figure sums.

20 Useful statistics

Period road tests are now readily available, but one question that all schoolboy car enthusiasts seem to want to know the answer to is "How fast is it Mister?" Well the TR2/3/3A were certainly no rockets by today's standards, but, compared to their contemporaries, these models could achieve the magic 100mph as shown on the speedometer, with the TR3A being just that little bit faster through the gears due to the bigger 2138cc engine. The 0 to 60mph time of the TR2 was also pretty good by the standards of the day, with just under 12 seconds being about the best time recorded, and it was actually quicker than the heavier TR3 fitted with a hardtop. Fuel consumption with overdrive was also pretty good considering the cars weighed 2100lb and 2464lb respectively. All the following data is for the TR2 unless stated.

Engine: Four cylinders, overhead valves, pushrod operated
Cubic capacity: 1991cc/121in^3, bore 83mm/3.268in, stroke 92mm/3.622in. Or 2138cc/130in^3, bore 86mm/3.386in, stroke 92mm/3.622in
Compression ratio: 8.5:1 (TR3A 9.1:1, TR3B 9.0:1)
Valve timing: Inlet valve opens at 150 before top dead centre and exhaust valve closes at 150 after TDC. Rocker clearances to be set at 0.010in/0.25mm inlet and 0.012in/0.3mm exhaust on earlier cars, and 0.010in/0.25mm inlet and exhaust on later cars with aluminium rocker pedestals. Note: All settings when cold.
Fuel system: Non-pressurised fuel tank with AC mechanical fuel pump and filter set at 1¼-2¼lb/in^2. Twin 1½in SU H4 carburettors on low-port head. Some TR3s and all TR3As were fitted with twin 1¾in SU H6 carburettors.

Dimensions
Overall length: 12ft 7in/3840mm
Width: 4ft 7.5in/1410mm
Height: 4ft 2in/1270mm (with hood up)
Wheelbase: 7ft 4in/2240mm

Track
Front: 3ft 9in/1140mm
Rear: 3ft 9.5in/1160mm
Ground clearance: 6in/152mm
Turning circle: 32ft/9.75m

Weights
Dry: 1848lb/838.2kg (TR3A 2050lb/929.8kg)
Max gross weight: 2105lb/955kg

Capacities	Imperial	Metric	USA
Fuel tank	12.5 gallons	57 litres	15 gallons
Engine sump	11 pints	6.25 litres	13.2 pints
Gearbox	1.5 pints	0.85 litres	1.8 pints
O/D gearbox	3.5 pints	2.0 litres	4.2 pints
Rear axle	1.5 pints	0.85 litres	1.8 pints
Cooling system	13 pints	7.4 litres	15.6 pints
inc heater	14 pints	8.0 litres	16.8 pints

Tyres & pressures
5.50 x 15, front 22lb/in^2, rear 24lb/in^2

Ignition system
Coil: Lucas B12 (TR3A HA12)
Distributor: Lucas DM2 P4 with centrifugal advance and vacuum retard
Contact breaker gap: 0.015in/0.4mm
Firing order: 1-3-4-2
Sparkplugs: Champion L10S with 0.032in/0.8mm gap
Ignition timing (fully retarded): 4 degrees BTDC

Electrical system
Voltage: 12-volt positive earth. 35-amp fusebox
Dynamo: Lucas C39PV/2 (TR3A Lucas C40-1)
Control box/regulator: Lucas RB 106/1 or RB106/2
Battery: Lucas GTW7A/2 or GTW9A/2 (7- and 9-plate cells respectively), 38 or 51 amp hour, with either a 4- or 5-amp charging rate

Starter motor: Lucas M 418 G
Flasher unit: Lucas FL2 (TR3A FL5)
Fuel and temp gauges: Smiths bi-metal resistance 10-volt system

Braking system
Lockheed hydraulic twin bore system (TR3/3A Girling CV Type, from chassis no TS13101)
Front brakes: 10in x 2¼in drums (TR3 front brakes 11in Girling disc from chassis no TS13101)
Rear brakes: 9in x 1¾in drums* (TR3 rear brakes 10in x 2¼in Girling HL3 drums)

* later changed on the TR2 to 10in x 2¼in drums from TS 5443

21 Troubleshooting

Below are some typical symptoms you may encounter, together with their probable causes and potential remedies.

Engine

Symptom	Possible cause	Potential remedy
Engine will not crank	There is a fault in the starting system	Refer to section on electrics
Engine cranks slowly	Engine oil too thick, stiff engine after rebuild or engine partially seized	Drain and replace oil, strip engine and replace parts as required
Engine cranks but does not start	Fault in ignition system, fault in fuel system, incorrect valve timing, compression leak	Re-time the engine, check head gasket
Engine starts but only runs for short periods	Air leak in manifold or blockage in exhaust	Trace and seal leak, remove blockage
Engine misfires at low speed	Fault in ignition or fuel systems, air leak in manifold or poor valve seating	Trace and seal leak, regrind valves
Engine misfires at high speed	As above but valve(s) may be sticking	Free valve(s) and trace cause
Engine misfires on acceleration	As above but investigate for broken valve spring(s)	Trace and replace spring(s)
Rough idle	Leaking head gasket, incorrect tappet clearances, worn cylinder bores	Replace gasket, adjust tappets, replace pistons and rings
Excessive oil consumption	Leaking oil seal, worn valve guides or piston rings	Replace seal and/or guides, fit new piston rings
Excessive fuel consumption	Fault in fuel system	Refer to fuel page
Pinking	Fault in fuel or ignition systems	Refer to those pages

Ignition system

Symptom	Possible cause	Potential remedy
Engine cranks but does not start	Battery discharged or defective, contact breaker points failure, sparkplugs defective	Recharge or replace battery, clean or replace points and/or sparkplugs
Engine starts but only runs for short periods	Possible short to earth or loose connection	Check plug leads and all connections
Engine misfires at low speed	Wrong type of sparkplug fitted	Clean, re-gap or replace sparkplugs
Engine misfires at high speed	Open circuit or loose connection in LT circuit	Trace and rectify
Engine misfires on acceleration	Plug leads connected wrongly	Check firing order
Rough idle	Static timing incorrect	Re-time ignition
Engine runs rough at high speed	Contact breaker points failure	Replace points
Lack of power	Coil or capacitor breaking down	Replace coil or capacitor
Poor acceleration	Open circuit or loose connection in LT circuit	Trace and rectify
Poor top speed	HT circuit broken in distributor due to damp	Clean and dry distributor cap
Excessive fuel consumption	Vacuum advance not working or worn distributor	Rectify or replace
Pinking	Using wrong grade of fuel	Boost the octane rating to 98-100

Lubrication and cooling system

Symptom	Possible cause	Potential remedy
Excessive oil consumption	Worn pistons and rings, worn valve guides, leaking crank oil seal or oil filter and cooler	Rebore, hone and fit new oversize pistons and rings, replace valve guides and /or seals
Low oil pressure	Faulty gauge, pressure switch or relief valve, worn oil pump or oil pick up blocked, damaged main or big end bearings, crank oil seal defective	Test and replace as required, replace oil pump, check crank and renew main bearings as required, replace oil seal

Overheating	Lack of coolant, thermostat jammed, fanbelt slipping, radiator core clogged with debris, water pump failure	Check coolant level, replace thermostat, check fanbelt tension, clean and flush radiator core, replace water pump
Engine fails to get to temperature	Thermostat jammed open	Replace thermostat

Clutch and gearbox

Symptom	Possible cause	Potential remedy
Clutch slipping	Clutch plate face worn, broken pressure plate	Replace clutch plate, replace clutch cover
Clutch will not disengage	Air in hydraulic system, too much play in release linkage	Bleed system, adjust or renew worn parts
Clutch judder	Clutch plate warped	Replace clutch plate
Clutch noise, squeal	Release bearing breaking up	Replace bearing
Clutch noise, rattles or chatter when idling or engaging clutch	Loose clutch or drive plate	Replace clutch
Car jumps out of gear when accelerating	Worn layshaft	Rebuild gearbox
Gearbox makes rattling noise	Synchromesh cones worn	Rebuild gearbox
Overdrive won't engage	Break in electrical circuit, failure of o/d oil pump	Check all wiring, check the detent switches on the top cover are adjusted properly, check oil level in gearbox and repair pump if required
Overdrive solenoid works but overdrive doesn't	Solenoid not actuating the lever correctly	Check adjustment on solenoid lever

Fuel system

Symptom	Possible cause	Potential remedy
Engine cranks but does not start	No fuel or fuel line blocked, defective fuel pump, carburettor needle valve jammed	Fill tank, blow through fuel line, check pump diaphragm and replace if necessary, check carburettors

Engine starts but only runs for short periods	Blockage in carburettor, idling speed too low, air filter clogged	Clean out carburettor, raise idling speed, clean or change air filters
Engine misfires at low or high speeds	Fuel pump defective, blockage or water in carburettor	Replace pump, clean out carburettor
Engine misfires on acceleration	Incorrect setting of choke control, incorrect float setting, air leak at manifold, throttle linkage poorly set up	Reset choke, reset float level, trace air leak and seal, reset linkage
Lack of power	Carburettor piston sticking, wrong jets fitted in carburettor	Oil carburettors and check damper levels, fit the correct jets
Poor acceleration	Water in carburetto, carburettor icing, incorrect grade of fuel	Drain out water and dry carburettor, wait for ice to melt. DO NOT use external heat source! Add higher octane fuel
Poor top speed	Blockage in carburettor, incorrect carburettor settings	Clean carburettor, reset choke/ fuel/ float levels and linkages
Excessive fuel consumption	Carburettor accelerator pump defective, wrong jets fitted, air filter clogged	Trace faults and rectify, clean air filters
Pinking	Incorrect grade of fuel, incorrect ignition timing	Fill tank with higher grade of fuel, re-time ignition
Backfire	Erratic fuel flow, incorrect choke setting, air leak at manifold	Check for blockage in fuel lines, reset choke, trace air leak and seal

Steering

Symptom	Possible cause	Potential remedy
Steering is stiff	Lack of lubricant in steering gear, incorrect steering geometry, uneven tyre pressures, wheels out of alignment	Grease steering, check geometry, check tyre pressures, adjust toe in and camber angles
Steering feels loose	Worn steering joints	Check all ball joints and steering couplings
Wheel shimmy	Slack wheel bearings, loose wheel nuts, steering rack loose	Check all wheel bearings, tighten steering rack mountings if loose and check all road wheel nuts and wire wheel splines are torqued up correctly
Car pulls to one side	Brakes pulling to one side, shock absorbers defective, broken spring, chassis frame twisted	Check brakes, springs and shock absorbers mountings, carry out drop check on chassis
Excessive tyre wear	Wrong tyre pressures, wheels out of balance or alignment, worn steering joints	Check pressures, replace tyres and get wheels balanced, check steering joints

Brakes

Symptom	Possible cause	Potential remedy
Brake failure	Fluid leak, seized brake pistons, air in the system, defect in master cylinder	Check for leaks at all unions, free and clean pistons, bleed brakes, replace master cylinder
Brakes ineffective	Worn brake pads and/or linings, worn or scored discs and/or drums	Replace all as required
Brakes grab to one side	Loose calliper or back plate, sticking wheel cylinder or calliper piston	Check and tighten bolts accordingly, free off piston(s)
Rear brakes binding on	Broken spring on drum	Check and replace
Spongy brake pedal	Air in the system, low brake fluid, calliper(s), master or wheel cylinder(s) defective	Bleed system, top up fluid, replace parts as required
Excessive pedal travel	Brake servo failure, wear in linkage, callipers or wheel cylinder defective	Replace defective parts

Hard to press pedal	Brake servo failure, wear in pedal linkage, blockage in pipework	Check servo vacuum hose for leaks, replace servo, check pedal mechanism, clear blockage
Brake squeal	Pistons in callipers or cylinder seized, brake pads not returning	Free up pads/linings and clean, grease shim plates with Copper Ease
Shuddering under braking	Callipers or back plates loose, disc(s) scored or warped	Check fixing bolts and tighten, replace discs if needs be
Handbrake ineffective	Brake shoes worn or badly adjusted, brake drums worn, cables worn	Check and either adjust or replace parts

Electrical equipment

Symptom	Possible cause	Potential remedy
Starter fails to crank engine	Battery discharged, starter motor solenoid defective, starter pinion jammed in ring gear	Charge or replace battery, replace starter motor, remove starter motor and check operation and condition of ring gear
Starter only cranks engine slowly	Battery discharged, bad earth, pre-engaged starter unit failing	Charge or replace battery, check earthing, replace starter motor
Ignition warning light remains on above idle speed	Loose connection, fanbelt broken or slack, dynamo defective	Check wiring, replace or tighten fanbelt, check dynamo brushes and connections, replace dynamo if necessary
Ignition warning light doesn't come on	Battery discharged, bad earth, broken or loose connection(s), bulb burned out	Recharge or replace battery, trace bad connection(s), replace bulb
Ignition warning light stays on even when engine is turned off	Ignition switch defective, dynamo defective	Replace switch, check dynamo wiring
Headlights dim	Dynamo defective, light switch defective	Check brushes, replace dynamo if necessary, replace light switch
Headlights stuck on dip or main beam	Dip switch broken	Check for loose connection, otherwise replace
Indicators malfunction	Faulty flasher unit, bad earth connection(s)	Replace flasher unit, check all earth connections

Although these cars are not within the scope of this book, it would be remiss of me not to mention them as they share so much of the mechanical side with the TR cars. All three cars are very rare today, and consequently command very high prices.

The TR2 Francorchamps

The Francorchamps was basically a TR2 with a fixed head coupé body conversion, complete with revised doors to enable wind-up windows to be fitted. Only 22 cars were built by the Imperia factory at Nessonvaux in Belgium. Standard TR2s were supplied

there in CKD form, and were modified according to customers' tastes and preferences. Mechanically, they followed the standard TR2 format, but there were some changes to internal fittings as a result of having full-size doors. These are very rare today, with only about 11 known survivors.

The Italia 2000 GT

The Italia 2000 GT was a very different attempt at producing a fixed head coupé on the TR3 chassis. It was styled by Giovanni Michelotti for Salvatore Ruffino, Triumph's Italian importer. It was produced from 1959 to 1962.

TRIUMPH "Coupé Francorchamps,,

22.1: The Franchorchamps fixed head coupé. A forerunner of the later windy window TRs.

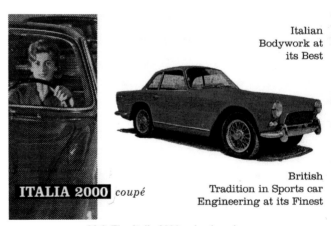

Italian Bodywork at its Best

ITALIA 2000 coupé

British Tradition in Sports car Engineering at its Finest

22.2: The Italia 2000 sales brochure.

22.3: The plush interior of an Italia 2000.

22.4: The author's very rusty ex-works Italia chassis No 1 that he found in a lock-up garage near Telford.

Unfairly described by some as a 'TR3 in a party frock,' the cars were hand-built at Vignale. They were very expensive compared to a normal TR, and the introduction of Triumph's own TR4, also styled by Michelotti, effectively put paid to the project. Most of the cars were sold in Europe and the USA, with fewer than half a dozen making it to the UK in RHD form. Potential customers in the USA had to sign an indemnity stating that, in the event of an accident, they knew spares for the body would not be available!

The total number of cars produced is not actually known as the build records have been lost, but the figure is generally reckoned to be about 300 or so. The author was once lucky enough to purchase chassis No 1 to save it from being scrapped, and, although he wasn't able to do this himself, the car is now finally being restored.

Some years ago TR enthusiast Paul Gerring and Revington TR embarked on a joint venture to commission a completely new car. They are now able to produce a brand new Italia for you if you should wish to own one. Without a doubt the Italia 2000 is the prettiest of all the TR derivatives ever made. Indeed, the shape of the body was later refined by Michelotti, and the Italia's influences on the Maserati Sebring 3500 GT can be clearly seen.

Apart from a slightly different radiator being fitted, mechanically the car is to standard TR3A specification. Had it been produced with the equally rare 'Sabrina' twin cam engine, then perhaps the car's 'TR3 in a party frock' sobriquet wouldn't have been coined, as that really would have made it stand out. As it is the cars command very high prices, with some now being valued at £100,000.

22.5: The 'Yellow Peril' that was commissioned by Paul Gerring and which featured many Revington TR modifications.

The Swallow Doretti

The Swallow Doretti was another car that used Triumph mechanicals, but this time mounted on a different chassis and body. The project used tubular steel for the main chassis members, and the car was built at the old Walsall Airport factory, which was part of the Tube Investments Ltd empire, in 1954/5.

Inspired very much by the Ferrari 166MM roadster, the car was 7in longer than a TR2, had a decent size boot, and even though it cost nearly £150 more, it presented Triumph's TR2 and Jaguar's XK140 with some real competition. However, corporate business was never going to allow such a thing, and Tube Investments was reportedly 'leaned

22.6: A Swallow Doretti competing at a TR Register sprint meeting at Curborough in 1978.

on' by Sir William Lyons of Jaguar to stop supplying Swallow with steel tube to build the chassis.

The car was squarely aimed at the American market, and was named after Dorothy Deen, a Californian Triumph dealer. Approximately 270 cars were built, and today they, too, command high prices.

Both the Francorchamps and the Italia offered expensively styled factory finished coupés on TR2/3 mechanicals. However, in keeping with the 1950s it was possible to convert your open topped TR into a closed coupé version by the addition of a large fibreglass moulding. It's not known how many of these conversions were carried out, and the author has only ever seen one other example of 'fastback' styling on a TR3.

Who made this car is another mystery, but no doubt a search of motoring magazines from the era would provide the answer. The styling might not be to everyone's taste, but it presaged a forthcoming trend for GT cars that would be taken up by Dove's of Wimbledon who produced a similar hatchback on the TR4. The concept was later copied with much greater success by arch rival MG with its MGB GT.

22.7: It is not known who made this coupé conversion of a TR3 or took the photograph, but it is certainly an interesting derivative and would be sought-after by collectors today.

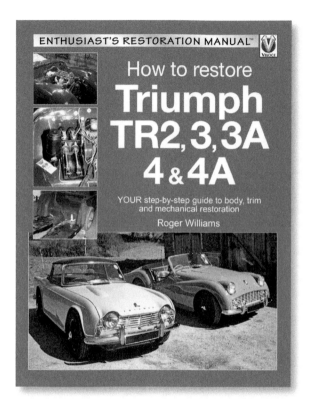

This book, which covers all Triumph TR2, 3, 3A, 4 & 4A models, explains the characteristics of the different models, what to look out for when purchasing and how to restore a TR cost effectively.

ISBN: 978-1-845849-47-4 • Paperback • 27x20.7cm • 208 pages • 500 pictures

For more information and price details, visit our website at www.veloce.co.uk • email: info@veloce.co.uk • Tel: +44(0)1305 260068

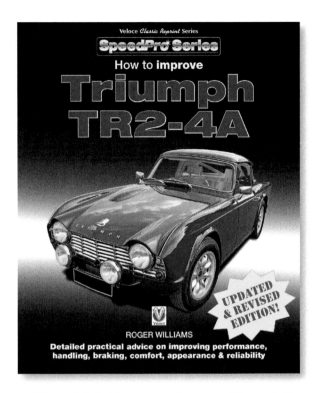

Aided by top racing and high-performance TR specialists, his own experiences, and those of other amateur restorers, the author explains in some detail how to increase the performance and handling of the four-cylinder TR sports cars for fast road, track days, or more serious motorsport.

ISBN: 978-1-787110-91-5 • Paperback • 25x20.7cm • 176 pages • 552 pictures

For more information and price details, visit our website at www.veloce.co.uk • email: info@veloce.co.uk • Tel: +44(0)1305 260068

Also from Veloce Publishing –

If you are a prospective buyer of a TR2 or TR3 this book will take you by the hand – from deciding whether a TR2/TR3 is for you, to choosing how and where to buy the best example. It contains a detailed and illustrated examination of sample cars, and is written by an expert with the sole aim of helping you make an informed choice.

ISBN: 978-1-787112-72-8 • Paperback • 19.5x13.9cm • 64 pages • 98 pictures

For more information and price details, visit our website at www.veloce.co.uk • email: info@veloce.co.uk • Tel: +44(0)1305 260068

Other books in this series –

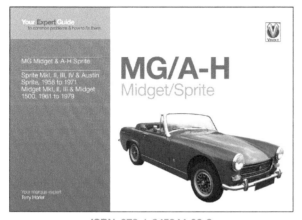

ISBN: 978-1-845844-02-8

ISBN: 978-1-787111-16-5

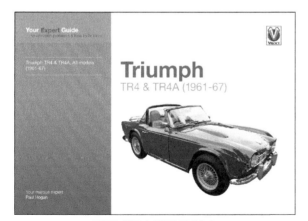

ISBN: 978-1-787115-64-4

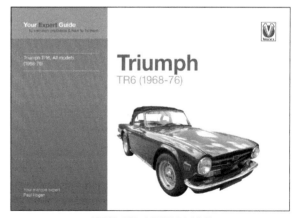

ISBN: 978-1-787114-19-7

Index